GROWING YOUR PROFESSIONAL PRACTICE

HAVE had a professional association with Vivienne Corcoran during the past 20 years. This association has embraced four quite different professional consulting firms, operating in markets as diverse as accounting, consulting, executive search and the law.

In all situations, Vivienne's professional work and advice has been clear, concise, logical and, above all, practical. There is a professional consistency to Vivienne's work, as the same general principles apply regardless of the speciality or nature of the professional practice.

What Vivienne has done in this book is to document her 'how-to' and working guide to growing a professional practice. When she has conducted workshops for me and my teams, Vivienne has always set the agenda to include what is now the subject matter of this book. Vivienne has taken us into her mind and exposed us to her own professional intellectual property.

This book identifies and details the major matters necessary for a professional firm to grow its revenue line. It is done in a concise and practical way, and encourages the practitioner to apply the principles recommended. All chapters are important for growing the revenue of a professional practice; but each practice will find some chapters more relevant than others, depending upon their stage of development.

I commend this book to you.

PETER C JOYCE
Chairman,
Dibbs Abbott Stillman I Lawyers, Melbourne

Chairman,
The Insight Group

GROWING YOUR PROFESSIONAL PRACTICE

Published in Australia by Marketing Logic Pty Ltd
Address: GPO Box 3206 Melbourne VIC 3001
Tel: 0417 567 506
Email: vivienne@marketinglogic.com.au
Website: www.marketinglogic.com.au

marketing
Logic

First published in Australia 2008
© 2016. Marketing Logic.

National Library of Australia Cataloguing-in-Publication entry
Corcoran, Vivienne
Growing Your Professional Practice: The How To Manual
ISBN: 9780646497297

Illustrations by Justin Garnsworthy www.justingarnsworthy.com.au

Disclaimer

All care has been taken in the preparation of the information herein, but no responsibility can be accepted by the publisher or author for any damages resulting from the misinterpretation of this work. All contact details given in this book were current at the time of publication, but are subject to change.

The advice given in this book is based on the experience of the individuals. Professionals should be consulted for individual problems. The author and publisher shall not be responsible for any person with regard to any loss or damage caused directly or indirectly by the information in this book.

GROWING YOUR PROFESSIONAL PRACTICE
THE HOW-TO MANUAL

VIVIENNE CORCORAN

ILLUSTRATIONS: JUSTIN GARNSWORTHY

marketing
Logic

Contents

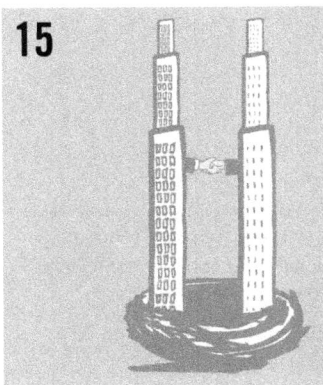

15

31

81

Dedication

f I know anything about professional services it is what I have learnt from the literally thousands of professionals I have worked with over the years. There are too many people to acknowledge and thank them all – suffice to say, if you have worked with me, I have learned from you, and thank you.

There are some organisations and people, though, who require special mention. At Mercer, I learnt that listening to what clients want can enable you to communicate and realise the value of almost any service. At Arthur Andersen I learnt the value of sheer hard work, and saw first-hand the power of true intelligence and networks. More recently, I have been privileged to work with a fabulous team at Pitcher Partners. For putting up with me and letting me ply my trade with them, I owe them thanks for their forbearance and patience. To Ian, Tim, Don, Gess and Alicia, many thanks.

More specifically, to Megan, Helen, Erin and earlier Tammy and Jo, my thanks for the support and laughter. To my team at Marketing Logic, both now and over the years, thank you to Devra, Kylie, Georgia, Natalie and Erica, without whom this book would never have made it out of my head. Importantly, thanks to my good friend, colleague and critic Mel. Many thanks to David Clemson for his professional wisdom and advice.

In the end, though, I must dedicate this book to my closest allies, my staunchest critics and my fabulous support crew, my family, without whom I would never have had the time or energy to put finger to keyboard.

To Ross, Adam and Luke, with love.

Introduction

Professionals are a particular type of beast and the practices they develop are particular as a result. Over more than 20 years in business I have worked with all types of professionals: accountants, doctors, lawyers, barristers, engineers, architects, IT recruiters, consultants, surgeons. While the work they do and the way they do it varies, there are still some major characteristics that they have in common that make a difference to how they work.

The main difference is that more than any other organisation a professional practice is literally a group of people – people with a passion for what they do.

Some practices are completely driven by consensus, some are more autocratic, others are completely corporate. Regardless of the final decision-making processes though, professional firms are driven by the people who put them together and the principals who continue that work. This means that regardless of the level of enthusiasm or skill of your staff or executive, nothing will happen effectively unless you have a principal who is both keen and able to drive the process. You can delegate work not enthusiasm, so try and focus on those things that have the principals' agreement or you will be wasting your time.

INTRODUCTION

Definitions

This is a handbook designed to help professionals grow their practices. It is not a theoretical treatise, it is very much a working guide based on my years working with professional service firms.

Being professionals, designed to think and taught to question (or perhaps the other way around), every reader will want some definitions, and although this is not that sort of book, here are a few.

Professional: if you have qualified in a profession – be it law, accounting, engineering, architecture, medicine or any other – and you are charging money for your services, then you are in a professional service.

Firms: you might call yourself a partnership, a consultancy, a business, a firm, etc. What you call yourself does not matter, in this book I use the term 'firm' to cover all of these structures. Also for this purpose, I use the term 'principal' to cover partners, directors, owners or whoever takes final responsibility for the service provided. 'Managers' refers to the next level of managers, directors or senior associates.

Size: the principles of this book have been distilled from years working with firms of all sizes and persuasions – large firms, small firms, one-man bands, city, suburban and regional firms, firms that have been in existence before you were born.

You: although for sake of simplicity and clarity this book addresses 'you' the readers, realistically all these guidelines (for they are guidelines and not rules) also apply to me as a professional. In the end, the same advice I offer to you I have used myself, not just on my long-suffering clients, but also on my own business.

Timing: There is no right or wrong time to buy, read or apply a book like this – you can start at any point and dip in and out as you need to.

1 Planning

A business plan, strategic plan, marketing plan: whatever you call it, you must have one – a picture of what you want to achieve and some simple steps to get there.

THERE ARE hundreds of books written about business planning – this is not one of them. Whether you call your plan a strategic plan, a business plan or, in many instances, a marketing plan, does not matter. The important thing is to get down and do the planning! You can argue later about what the plan is called and what other plans you need to make it work.

The keys to all effective planning remain the same:
- set simple goals – where you want to get to
- agree on a plan of action – now that you know what it is you are trying to achieve, you need to work out how to cover the distance between where you are now and where you want to go
- write them down (you would be surprised how many relatively large businesses have plans that live in people's heads), and
- follow-up – make sure the plan does not gather dust but is used as a real driver of the business.

Getting started

If you do not have a business plan, then it is important to at least get started. Business plans do not need to be long, lavish MBA-polished documents. In fact, they rarely work when they are. What you need is the equivalent of a recipe for a good meal or a great drink. You need to have a picture of what you want to achieve and then some simple steps to get there.

> As with recipes, the plan's format will depend on your taste and experience. Some people like pictures, some like diagrams, some like lots of plain text without pictures. The format is not important; PowerPoint, Word, dot-point or narrative all depend on you and your business colleagues.

You must decide what form you want the business plan to take, how often you are going to refer to it and who is going to be responsible for keeping it updated. Ideally the business plan needs to be in a form accessible and comprehensible to everyone who needs to contribute to it.

There are five main elements a business plan needs to contain:
1. Background to the business (how it started, why it started and what it set out to achieve)
2. Organisation goals (what it stands for and wants to be known for)
3. Long-term goals (fees, profit, size, specialisations)
4. Short-term goals (what you need to achieve first), and
5. Action plans (who will do what, when and how).

TABLE 1: A SAMPLE PLANNING TIMEFRAME			
Plans	Goals	Involving	Review
Firm/strategic	Establish an industry group	Principals	1–3 years
Long-term	Grow by 5%	Principals and principals-elect	5 years
Short-term	Boost experience/credentials in a specialist tax area	Divisional principals and managers	6 months

The following chapters will work through these goals and action plans. Read them before you start the business plan.

A schedule needs to be set for reviewing progress against action plans and updating the business plan (see Table 1). The timeframe for this will be driven by your business, the market in which you operate, and the effort required to do the updating. If you set the frequency of updating too often it becomes an endless, repetitive task that no-one will want, and the changes since the last review will be meaninglessly small. If the timeframe is too long, then everyone will have forgotten what you set out to achieve and you will often find yourselves going over old ground.

Make someone responsible for implementing this review process, perhaps the managing partner. A retired partner or consultant can also be effective and less likely to be distracted by the day-to-day business. Schedule in days/half days for each of these activities at least six months in advance – this will give you a line in the sand to work towards.

Tying the planning process into the professional review process can also be an effective way of keeping everyone focused on getting the planning done!

S.M.A.R.T.

For your plans to really work, they need to be a number of things:

Short: unless your goals are short and memorable then they will be difficult to achieve.

Measurable: you need to determine when, by whom and against which criteria your plans will be measured.

Appropriate/achievable: setting achievable plans means you avoid disappointment later.

Relevant: goals set are relevant to your firm and where you want to be.

Timely: all plans must have a timeframe within which they can be measured.

Reporting

Monthly reporting against the action plan at divisional level with quarterly bigger-picture reviews is helpful. The financial controller can be responsible for reporting against financial criteria but the larger issues of reputation and skill sets will not be able to reported against from the financial system. If a goal is to be measurable, then you need to determine the criteria by which they will be measured. These may be:

- client surveys
- staff surveys, and
- industry benchmarks, reports, research or analysis.

Be careful that you do not set criteria that are more complicated or expensive to measure than the plan itself warrants!

The most important thing to do with plans is to *get started*!

WHAT TO DO NOW
- [ ] If you have a business/marketing plan – revise it.
- [ ] If you don't – write one.
- [ ] Make sure your plan contains:
  - background to the business
  - goals that are SMART
  - organisational goals
  - long-term and short-term goals, and
  - action plans that are measurable and can be reported against.
- [ ] If unsure, check Chapter 2.

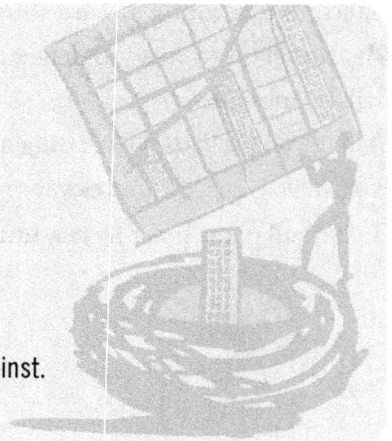

2 Setting goals

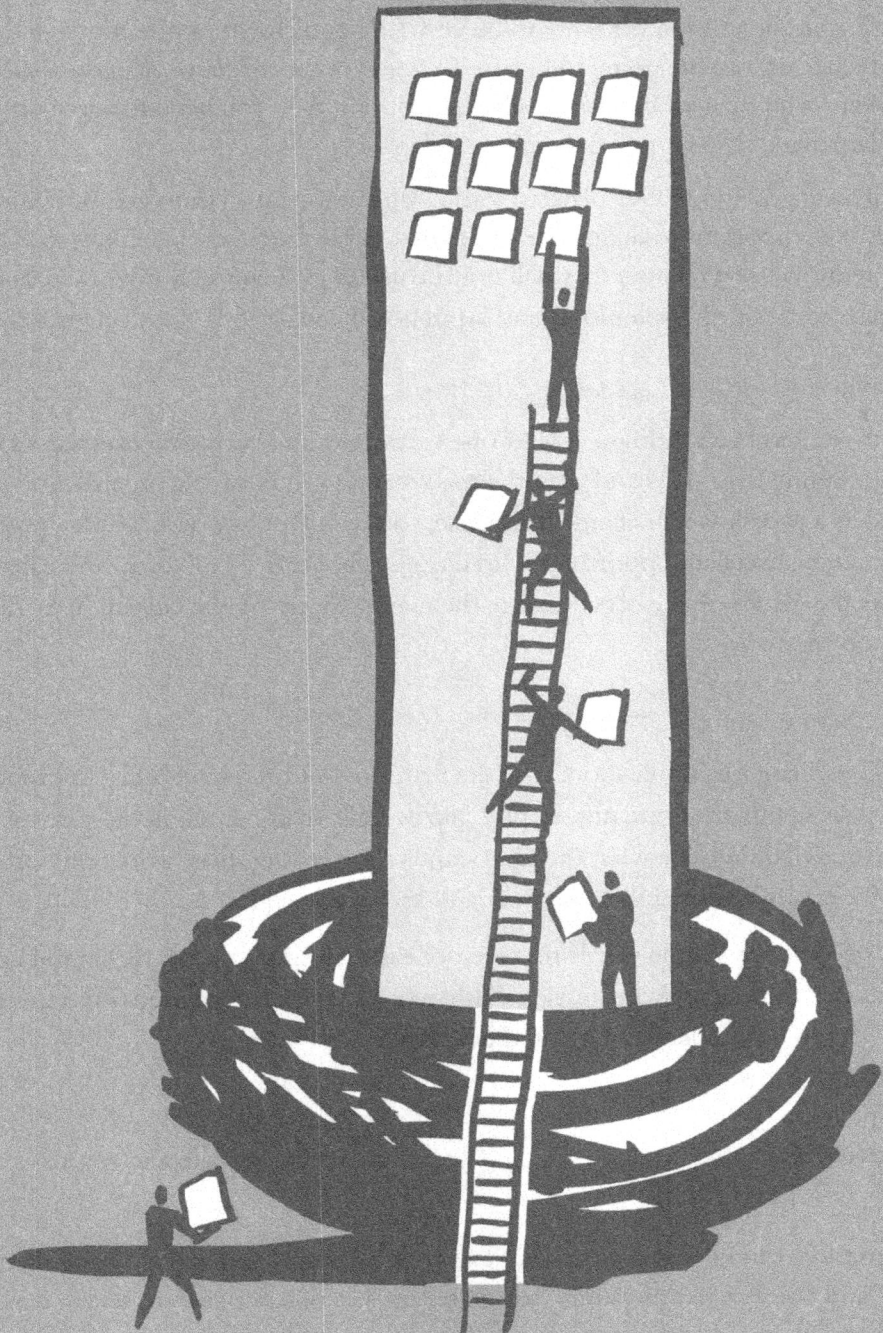

Define your values; describe your firm's 'personality' as if it were a person. Then you have the foundation for your goals — where you want to go.

N PROFESSIONAL practices where all the principals think they are their own boss, it is not uncommon for there to be very little agreement on the fundamentals of the practice. If you are going to be one firm and not a collective of individuals running their own practices but essentially sharing rent, then you need to agree on the core fundamentals of your practice: values and goals.

Goal setting is an obvious place to start — where do you want to go? But before you set goals it is important to define the values that guide the practice. Unless your goals support and reinforce your values, they will only be useful as financial hurdles. Goals based on values can be both inspirational and aspirational and serve as a rallying call for the firm.

Develop a list of agreed values for the firm

Everyone has been through at least one corporate soul-searching exercise where you set out to define the values and then the mission and vision of the organisation. If you saw these as a pointless management exercise, you would not be alone. Done properly, though, they can be excellent opportunities to engage with staff of all levels and listen to what they see as the values of the organisation, the major drivers of the culture. Why did they join, why do they stay?

What do you stand for as a practice?

This is a chance to think about why the firm exists. Often it will exist in order to be things that your competitors are not, to fill a gap in skills or approach in the market. Write a list of words that describe what the firm stands for. Getting these words out into the open can greatly improve your ability to attract and keep good staff.

You need to use simple words that are not easily misinterpreted. Be careful not to include platitudes; for example 'professional' is a word we take for granted — it does not add anything to our understanding of the firm. Do we value:

- inclusiveness
- openness
- excellence
- client focus
- caring
- practicality
- technical skill, and so on?

Often these can be vague terms that everyone feels embarrassed to discuss out loud, but ask staff and clients what they think you stand for as a practice and see which words they use.

What do you want to be known for?

What would you want clients to say about you to other prospective clients? All too often we find ourselves with a reputation we feel is not within our control. If a client were to say of your firm 'You should talk to Brown and Co, they are great at …', how would you like them to finish that sentence? Think not just about the immediate answer, but also what you would like them to say in the future.

Sometimes what you want to be known for will be a specific technical skill, it might be an attitude, it might be an industry. The key is to remember that what a client will say about you will be from their perspective not yours, so you need to understand what clients see as the real value of the service you provide. Agree on a simple sentence that describes what you do.

What is the practice's personality?

A practice, like an individual, can be seen as a collection of its traits. So are you approachable, commercial, technically brilliant? You need to make some conscious choices about how you want to be seen, which parts of your firm's 'personality' you most want to emphasise. Remember, you need to look at what attracts staff as well as clients.

Describe your firm's 'personality' as if it were a person. It may feel silly but it will be very useful later on:

> 'Brown and Co. is a progressive, flexible law practice with specific property law expertise …'
> 'Green and Co. is rigorously intelligent and unfailingly diligent.'

One of the best aspects, and one of the challenges, of professional practices is how personal they are. In many ways, clients engage with a professional practice as if it was one person or a group of people rather than as a company. For this reason, the selection of the people who will become the future leaders of your practice is critical.

Once people become principals it is too late to change their personalities or style of working. We need to work on making sure they fit and project the personality of the firm long before they reach the principal level. This does not mean that principals need to be clones – far from it; they need to be a well-balanced group who hold core beliefs and values in common.

Establish and agree goals

It is critical that all principals and managers responsible for contributing to the success of the organisation agree on the goals as set. It is too easy for the principals to set goals without really taking into account the opinions of the people who will be doing the work. If this is the first time you have set these sorts of goals, you may find there is more resistance than you thought, but eventually you need *all* the principals to agree on *all* the goals.

Get commitment from all principals/managers to the same goals

In a perfect world, or more relevantly, a perfect professional practice, everyone who joined the firm would have done so because they were attracted to its values and culture. During the recruitment and then induction process, the goals of the organisation would have been further explained to them.

In reality, this is far from the case. In these days of skills shortages, there are so many positions and so few professionals that we need to be careful what we assume about recruits.

Back to goals

What is the practice seeking to achieve in the short and the long terms? There are four important elements to consider:

- firm goals
- short-term goals
- long-term goals, and
- action plans.

Firm goals

One of the critical issues in both the marketing and management of professional firms is to remember there is a difference between the sole practitioner and the practice. Even when a firm only includes one practitioner, there is a difference between marketing yourself (Brenda Brown and Associates) and marketing a firm.

AN ASIDE – WORKING WITH THE NEXT GENERATIONS

THERE ARE a number of issues affecting what we now call 'employer choice'. Potential staff are better informed and more discerning than in previous generations. The internet provides them with instant access to information with which to compare firms. They also have more choice than in periods of higher unemployment and can afford to be fussier.

The current, and definitely future, generations of professionals will be able to gain more information from non-official than official sources. Recruits of all ages, but particularly graduates, are less likely to listen to what you say about your firm than what their friends and peer group say about your firm.

This means your reputation among your existing staff is critical to your ability to attract new staff. So you need to ensure staff are happy but also listen to what they think of you – because this is what they will say about you to their peers. You cannot get this sort of information through staff

surveys, paper or electronic. You need to listen to staff when they are at work, at play, stressed, relaxed, sober and drunk – this is what their friends will hear.

Much has been written about Generations Y, X and Z, but in my experience they all want to be favourite children, they think they are important and they want you to show that you think they are important too. This means asking, rather than expecting, them to do things and engaging with them more as equals than perhaps your early employers did with you.

In times of strong employment, almost all your staff could get another job somewhere else, so you need to give them reasons to stay. They see themselves giving their time and energy – they need to be asked and thanked and they will have varying levels of professional expertise that you need to tap into and help them improve.

With the end of the 'career for life' comes the need to provide more than a workplace and a pay packet to staff. You need

In some instances the market only buys the services of the firm because of the presence of the principal, whereas in others the difference is driven by your plans for the long-term future of the firm. These longer-term plans will affect everything from what you call the firm to the way in which you transact business.

- Do you want to take on partners?
- Do you want to be known as a multi-service, multi-skill-set firm?
- Do you want to sell or pass on the firm when you retire?

If the answer to these questions is yes, then you need to develop goals for the firm that are more than just your personal goals.

If the answer is no, and regardless of the number of staff you have you plan to remain the sole owner of the business, then you need to look at your own personal goals before you can develop goals for the firm.

Your personal goals

If there is more than one of you in the business, then you need to ensure everyone sees the difference between their own individual goals and those of the firm. Both sets of goals are critical, but the order in which they are established makes a difference to the way in which the overall plan will roll out. The principals' view of the firm should govern the order in which these goals are set.

to take account of the fact that your staff are working to live and not living to work. This does not mean being endlessly flexible in order to meet their desire for personal health or world peace, but rather being reasonable about providing work/life balance.

Equally important is providing balance within work as well. Staff need challenge and variety as well as technical backup and training. In many respects, because staff choose who they work for, workplaces become more important rather than less.

Seemingly small gestures like breakout spaces, fruit, social events and newspapers are as important as the traditional health club and childcare larger firms offer. Far from seeing these as elements only large firms can offer, talk to other local professional firms (perhaps in non-competing professions) and see what you can organise together. Look at local professional associations and/or larger professional firms and see if you can get together to deliver some of these typically 'larger firm' benefits.

Culture is also a critical issue; you will need to become more open and receptive and be seen to be democratic if younger generations are going to want to become a part of your team.

Finding alternatives to money and status as incentives will become increasingly important. You need to recognise and reward those members of staff who do not want to, or are unlikely to, become principals. You need to think hard about how to manage succession in your practice without asking younger staff to mortgage their houses to join you. For many, increasing debt for long-term gain is not an option, especially as they do not see themselves staying in the same job for the length of time it would take to realise this investment.

Consider other options – higher pay without dividends (the salaried partner model), share options and other structures that will attract and retain younger professionals.

If the practice is now, and is planned to always be, a single-principal practice, then the principal should set his or her own personal goals first before setting those for the firm. In this instance the firm is serving the principal, not vice versa. Unless the practice meets the principal's personal needs for income, satisfaction and balance then it is unlikely the practice will prosper.

If, on the other hand, the practice aims to be a multi-principal practice (regardless of whether or not it is at the moment) then it is important that you set the firm goals and the principals agree on them before each principal sets their own goals. Having each principal set their goals first and then making a set of firm goals around those will almost certainly guarantee the firm will pull apart sooner or later as individual goals diverge.

There are instances in which the principals' individual goals remain congruous throughout the full length of a firm's life, but this is rare. Even when this is the case, this extreme congruence makes it difficult to admit new principals to the firm and then to make the transition to the next generation.

Short-term goals

There will always be a number of short-term goals, that is, goals that can be achieved within a year. Given that these are the goals that will affect how much the principals earn in the next 12 months, these are the ones that are the easiest to fix everyone's attention on.

As a basic rule of thumb, I would start with short-term goals for the first year (and that may well be enough for the first five years of a firm's existence). Only once issues of sustainability have been resolved and there is at least a year's salaries and rent in the bank

TABLE 2: EXAMPLES OF VARYING GOALS

Area	Short-term	Long-term
Industry	Establish an industry group	Grow industry capability
Size	Grow by 5%	Achieve 10% growth each year
Services	Boost experience or credentials in a specialist tax area	Develop specialist tax practice
Recruitment	Hire extra staff	<15% staff turnover
Clients	Replace Major Lost Client & Co.	30% client referrals
Proposals	Win 10% more proposals	Win 70% of all proposals
Succession	Manage retirement of principal	Balance age groups throughout the practice
Fees	Grow by 5%	20% increase in fees each year
Profitability	Become profitable	30%
Reputation	Attract new tax work	Be seen as an expert in specialist tax

is it worth looking at longer-term goals. That said, it is important to have a longer-term vision of where the firm will be in five years time when you first start the business. This is used not so much as a meaningful goal as a basis against which to measure the relevance of the short-term goals.

The one-year action plan breaks the bigger picture down into steps for individuals or divisions to achieve towards the larger and longer-term organisational goal.

Long-term goals

These goals are driven more by where you want the practice to be at the end of five years than during the next year. They will contain a mixture of practical issues (such as size) and intangibles such as reputation – what does the organisation want to be known for in the long term?

Reputation is in many instances in the eye of the beholder. Most practices seek to develop a reputation for strong skills, good ethics, etc. These are best included as values that the practice and individuals can aspire to and measure themselves against and to which recruits can be attracted, rather than goals. More relevant from a marketing perspective are the reputational issues of which type of work, client, and skills you want to be known for.

Division goals

Certainly when a firm starts it is often easiest to ask each principal to set their projected financial goals and for the firm's goals to be a collation of those goals. This is manageable for the first year and perhaps for as long as the firm is only setting short-term goals.

As soon as you need long-term goals, then the firm needs to set the goals and the divisions need to decide how they are going to help meet those overall goals.

A few words of warning:

- Only the financial goals should be set by division. The longer-term service, reputation and positioning goals need to be set by the firm. Each division and principal needs to agree with these as the goals that guide the whole firm and must commit to upholding those goals from their division's point of view. There may be issues of specialisation or reputation that individual divisions will be more responsible for than others, but if there is to be a major push in any one direction then that needs to be a commitment made by the firm as a whole.
- Divisions can be *accountable* for certain goals but the whole firm must be *responsible* for them. Sheeting home the responsibility for achieving any one goal just to a division and its principals and staff will eventually divide the firm (or ensure it stays divided). Divisions need to ask for and receive help in achieving goals that contribute to the overall firm's goals. This includes sharing resources, ideas, clients and fees.
- New or growing divisions or practices within the firm need to be given time to build. Resources, funds, staff and even clients need to be donated to the cause if it is going to prosper.

Action plans

Goals are nothing without the plans to achieve them (see Table 3). You need to determine what actions are needed to achieve a particular goal, and then allocate responsibility for each action to a principal.

If you have someone who is a wiz at project management then get them to create a project plan by all means, but make sure it does not take longer to do the planning than it takes to do the actions. A principal needs to be in charge and hold everyone accountable for getting their actions completed and reporting to the principal group.

TABLE 3: EXAMPLES OF AN ACTION PLAN			
Goal	Action to achieve goal	Responsibility	Timeframe
Establish an industry group	Identify all people with industry experience	Greg	6 September
	Collate list of clients in industry	Allison	6 September
	Ask for details of experience in industry	Greg	6 September
	Investigate industry associations	Michael	12 September
	Meet to review industry experience	All	15 September

WHAT TO DO NOW
- [ ] Develop agreed firm values.
- [ ] Establish and agree goals:
  - set and agree firm goals;
  - understand everyone's personal goals;
  - set long-term goals;
  - commit to short-term goals; and
  - agree on division/business unit goals.
- [ ] Create and follow up on action plans.
- [ ] Put all these in your business plan.

3 Growing your practice through better client relationships

Your clients are partners in your future: they define your practice and how others see you. Make sure you know all there is to know about them.

N O DOUBT you decided to start a practice with people you admire and respect. In most instances, your clients will also come to the firm the same way, drawn by relationships and knowledge of the people involved. The same will be true of your first staff. In this way, at the beginning (and until the firm becomes big enough to be a well-known brand), any practice is you, your clients and your staff.

Partnerships are relationships

Your clients and staff define your practice and how others see you. This is the reason why you need to spend time each year looking at your clients and staff and making sure that they too embody the brand and positioning that you have determined for yourself.

The clients and staff you have, and the way they behave and describe your firm, is more important in the long term than the name or printed image of the brand.

Another reason you need to look closely at your client relationships is that your clients dominate your current work as well as your opportunities for the future. Clients are in many ways partners in your future. It is important that at every point in your relationship with a client you know as much about them as it is possible to know, and that you can be (reasonably) sure of what they would say about you if asked.

Building relationships

There are many ways of classifying clients, none better than any other. It is, however, important to remember the effect that classifications can have on both staff and, even worse, clients (see Class Action). So apart from calling them something acceptable, the main thing is to distil a manageable sublist of major clients you can really focus on.

These will be clients that are:
- profitable
- sustainable
- challenging, and
- good business partners – that is, clients that are of strategic importance to the firm.

The size of this 'major client list' will depend on the size of your firm. It needs to be large enough to sustain the firm if all the other clients left, but also small enough to be manageable. You need to be able to review this list monthly. In my experience, if any partner has more than 10 'critical' clients to manage monthly, then someone is going to get short-changed. These are the clients that you need to nurture. Other clients will come and

ONE FIRM classified its clients as A, B and C-class clients according to the level of ongoing fees they brought in. It only took a slip of the mail merge for all the clients to find out which 'class' they belonged to, with some embarrassing consequences.

The almost amusing postscript was that (having chastised the 'girl' who did the mail merge) the firm changed their categories to gold, silver and bronze. I am sure bronze class would have had much the same view as C-class clients of their relative importance!

go and each year this client list will change, but if these clients are your major assets, then you need to be able to see and manage them.

Understand client relationships

Now that you have a list of the clients that are critical to your business, review the relationships you have with them:

- Are they as strong as they could be?
- Where could they be improved?
- Is the relationship between two individuals or between two organisations?
- How deep do the relationships go?
- Could the relationship survive the change of a principal at either organisation?
- Have they referred you work?
- If not, why not?
- How much time do you spend with them discussing things other than the work you do together?
- How much do you know about their business and where it is going?

These are the type of questions you need to be able to answer for the major clients of your firm. You need to collate this information from principals, managers, other professionals who provide services to the client and from the clients themselves. You need to find a sensible way to document, store and retrieve this information (not in principals' heads!).

Understand clients' needs

When you start working through these type of questions, you will find there is quite a bit you do not know about your clients and what they think. In many instances this is normal and reflects the fact that we all tend to 'chat' rather than actually discussing issues of importance.

This is even more the case with questions that relate directly to their relationship with you. Issues such as which elements of your service are really important to them (for example: 'responsiveness', 'full service', partner access) are often things we only find out when the client is unhappy and leaves. It is important not to make assumptions.

TABLE 4: REASONS TO INTERVIEW CLIENTS

Excuses not to call	Reasons to call
Clients are too busy	No client has ever said they were too busy to talk to me.
Clients are not interested in what we do	Clients are paying good money for you to work for them and they not only notice but are interested.
Only someone who knows the client can ring	Provided the person who rings says they are ringing on your behalf, clients are always happy to talk. Clients will often feel more comfortable talking about you to someone else and it almost guarantees you will hear the truth.
You are not an accountant/lawyer/architect – only a 'professional' can interview clients	Clients have never asked which department I am from, they have never asked whether I am a 'professional', they take the interview at face value. Remember that these interviews are not about work, they are about relationships.
The client is not happy with us now, wait until later	This is the best time to talk to them – it shows you have nothing to hide and they may open up and you could resolve the issue faster.
The clients only know me	Most clients know more about the teams that work on their jobs than you think they do, they know their names, their skills, they care about them and are happy to talk about them.
They won't have anything to say	Clients love to be asked what they think, they love talking about their businesses, they often talk for hours!
You do not have a reason to talk to him	Again, this is a good time to talk because then you can talk about service and value rather than work.
I am too busy	This is a great time to use someone else who is less busy to make contact with your client.
I know what they think	I have never interviewed a client where the partner/principal did not learn something they did not know before the interview – don't make assumptions!
We do not have someone who can call the clients	If you are a sole practitioner, get someone else you trust, perhaps even your accountant or lawyer, to do it for you and you can return the favour for them.
I am uncomfortable with the idea of ringing and asking questions	This is the real reason most of us do not want to ring our clients. It is often harder to ring your own clients than someone you do not know. Get someone else to ring the client, the important thing is to find out what they think, not to replace you in their affections.

TABLE 5: EXAMPLES OF MARKET BASE QUESTIONS

Question	Rationale
Who else did you look at when you were looking for a provider and why?	This is where you find out who clients compare you to. This can sometimes be surprising, will probably change over time and will differ from discipline to discipline within the firm. These are the competitors you need to watch, not the ones **you** think are important.
Is there anything that distinguishes us from our competitors?	This is where it is important to listen for what clients think, and how they express it, not what you think. Often what you think sets you apart is not important to the client.
What keeps you with us?	Often a leading question, this is where clients will sometimes praise you for the work you have done already and indicate their concept of the value of what you offer. Otherwise it will tell you which clients need to be brought closer to the firm.
Is there anything that would make you leave us or any work you feel we could not do?	Again, this helps define you in the clients' terms and tells you which parts of your business you need to emphasise.
How do you describe your business/ organisation in terms of size/market segment?	The answer will help you describe your target market in their terms rather than yours. I have met firms who think they are servicing small clients when the clients think they are big!

TABLE 6: EXAMPLES OF SERVICE FEEDBACK QUESTIONS

Question	Rationale
What brought you to the firm?	Here we need to find out how and why the client came to our firm. What prompted them to look. Who referred them?
What are the issues of most importance to your business?	This is the 'what keeps you awake at night?' question. Clients usually love talking about their businesses and this gives them a chance to tell you what their major issues are, so you can make sure you address them. If you think there is something you can do to help them, then say so while you have them on the phone.
What do you see as the real value of working with us?	This is where you find out why the clients pay the bill. While I have had some discussion with clients about the amount of the bill, the real issue is the value rather than the cost. Knowing what they value can help you make sure the invoices reflect the value not just the fees.
Was there anything we should have done that we did not do?	Often a leading question, this is where clients will sometimes tell you of things that you could do (more fees) but often also praise you for the work you have done already (referrals, testimonials).
Is there any other work that we could be doing for you but are not?	For newer clients this is a chance for you to make sure they know about all the services you offer. For longer-term clients this is a chance to make sure you have as much of their work as possible or to find out why another provider is doing some of their work instead of you.
We hold client service meetings for all our major clients. Are any issues you think we should discuss?	This tells the client that they are important to you and gives you a chance to check that they get all the invitations and communications you send out and which ones are of interest.
(If response has been positive) We are often asked for referees who can talk about the work we do. Would you be a referrer?	This is a chance to get clients to tell you what they think, if they are not prepared to be a referee, then this is when you can find out why. If they are, it reminds them of their positive opinion of your firm and provides you with a good list of referrers when required.

If a client has raised an issue, then it is important that they see you have done something about it, otherwise they will feel as if the whole process was a PR exercise. In the area of client opinions, perception *is* reality.

Once you have decided the format that client documentation will take, make sure you keep the details of these interviews on file. If clients discuss some sensitive issues, then keep the documents password-protected, but be careful that you do not restrict access too far. These client interviews are only worth doing if you:

- listen with an open mind
- understand the issues from the client point of view
- pass the learning from the interview on to *all* those people involved with the client, and
- take action – and be seen to take action – on those issues that the client has raised.

The documentation will allow whoever does the interviews to confirm which interviews have been done, and to make sure they know what has been done on an issue before they talk to the client again.

Identify value

As we have already mentioned, the cost of professional services is usually reasonably easy to identify and quantify. The main issue for clients, though, is not the cost to you, but the value to them. It is always worth considering:

The real cost of services to the client

A client needs to earn sufficient income and profit in order to pay for your services. But the real cost to the client is more than the dollars on the invoice. Other things need to be factored into the equation:

- the cost of their time (both real and opportunity) spent working with you
- the cost of having you on their premises, perhaps disrupting the schedules of their staff, and
- the time and effort they need to spend sourcing data, finding information and answering your questions.

Think about these costs when you look at setting your fees.

The value you deliver

Much has been written, and even more discussed, over the past 20 years about the commoditisation of professional services. Audit fees, for example, continue to decline in real terms and the growth of 'fixed fee for service' providers does little to encourage a view of professional services as a good return on investment.

Have a look at the communication you provide to your clients – there are terms of engagement, retainer letters, terms and conditions, fee arrangements and schedules of rates. The delivery of these is standard before any work has been done. While the legal fraternity

KNOW WHAT YOUR CLIENT THINKS ABOUT YOU

A FIRM's managing partner told me that the single point of contact between the principal and the client was not only critical to the workings of the firm, it was what the clients valued above everything else. It was what set the firm apart from its competitors.

In conducting client interviews I spoke to a client who said that what he liked best about the firm was that he could ring a wide range of principals depending on the question he had and get an answer. He said what set the firm apart for him was the confidence it had in all of their principals to answer a question and then communicate between themselves what had happened.

If this firm had not asked clients what they thought, then it would have been very easy to go along, doing what they had always done and ignoring what the client really valued.

may consider this to be prudent, the fact is most of this 'communication' does nothing to encourage clients to think about value. It speaks only about cost. Have a look at all these documents as if you were receiving, not sending them.

What is the client going to get for the fees you charge? In simple terms the answer might be accounting, contracts, legal representation, designs; but these are commodities that the client could look at doing without, providing themselves or searching for the lowest-cost provider. If the answer instead was peace of mind, a strong basis upon which to value or finance the business or security of operation, then this is something that is not only valuable but also difficult to price and compare. You can get an alternative price on having your accounts done, but not on peace of mind.

While the general value of services will be much the same, there is also part of the value that is unique to the client, depending on their business and situation. The key is to identify, and make sure the client understands, that value.

The general value from professional services can be:

- peace of mind
- external advice
- board-level input
- professional expertise
- technical advice
- compliance, or
- legal protection.

It is important to remember that many of these types of value are, because of their general nature, taken for granted by clients. This is what they expect from a professional services provider, and this is what they think they are paying the high fees for.

The more specific value statements may include hints of this general value, but the key is to express it in more individual ways. This is perhaps where professionals have the most to learn. In my interviews with professional services firm clients, they have rarely found it hard to articulate the value of the relationship.

BEWARE THE EMAIL TRAP #1

WHILE email is a fabulous enabler, it can also be a convenient excuse for avoiding personal contact. In my conversations with professional service firm clients, very few have difficulty spelling out the value they get from their advisers.

While the actual work clearly differs and the value may differ in specific terms, certainly the major area in which clients get value is in personal contact with their advisers.

Much of the real value you deliver to clients happens not in the reports or results you deliver, but in the issues you mention in passing, the advice you are able to give on the spot.

This only really happens when we talk to clients face-to-face or, at the very least, on the phone. You can delegate and do work at arm's length, but in my experience value is only delivered in person.

A quick email can be a good way of passing information on, so send through links or emails but then keep a note of them and make sure you discuss them the next time you meet. This avoids wasting time and ensures that you discuss the issues concerned even if the client has deleted the emails!

Examples include:

'What I like about (the firm) is that although I own and run my business on my own, I can always ring and speak to one of the partners who works on my file and ask them a question or for an opinion. It is like having a board of advisers on tap.'

'The (specific) opinion is something I need to get from a regulatory point of view and they do a good job. The real value, though, comes from the list of things my staff and I could do better next year. It is as if I get a professional quality improvement program along with the compliance. I look forward to the list (of things we should be doing) changing every year, I want it to get longer not shorter.'

The key is to find the specific value of your service to each client and ensure they recognise and appreciate that value. It is important that each stakeholder understands and appreciates the value of the services throughout the lifetime of the engagement. For this, you need to take the individual into account when assessing the specific value.

It is easy to understand that individuals at different clients have different needs and perceptions of value. What we also need to remember is the same is true of different individuals *within the same client*. If we are going to protect the firm's client relationships from generational and management changes, then it is critical we develop and maintain relationships with more than one stakeholder at the client. Understanding the true nature of our client relationships is critical to your ability to grow and prosper.

WHAT TO DO NOW

- ☐ Analyse your client relationships.
- ☐ Ask what clients think.
- ☐ Understand what they need.
- ☐ Identify the value of what you do for the client.

4 Your target market

When you have your values, your goals and you know what your clients think of you, use what you know about them to drive your search for new business.

The first step is to review and analyse your existing client list. It is best to start with information you can get hold of rather than wait desperately for information you should have. Like the dentist's children, professional firms often have the worst reporting. Classify your clients according to some relevant criteria. These may include:

- fees – one-off, ongoing
- referrals in
- strength and depth of the relationship
- strategic importance to the firm
- how well they pay
- write-offs
- profitability;, and
- nternal characteristics – partner/industry/work type.

I have seen some very sophisticated analysis along these lines, much of it done by people with stronger mathematical skills than mine, but to be honest, the simpler the analysis the better. The main purpose is to determine which combination of clients and work best suits your firm – which ones you want more of. If you have developed a major client list (see Chapter 3), use that list.

From a long-term perspective you need to know what type of analysis you want so you can brief your IT and administrative staff on what your systems need to deliver.

In the short term, you need to work with what you have. It is more important to get started than for the data and the analysis to be perfect.

Define your target market

Who are you trying to market to? The analysis of your existing client base will provide some clues:

- which clients/work are the most profitable?
- which clients are the best payers?
- which clients refer the most work?

The first time you go looking for these answers you will probably need to find new ways of looking for the information – you will have to copy data from one place to another, look in diaries, and so on. Eventually, you need to get to the point where you have a system for getting this data on a regular basis.

USE DIFFERENT PERSPECTIVES TO IMPROVE THE MIX

WHEN I asked a firm these questions, we found some interesting answers. One director was unhappy with her existing client base because she did not like working for doctors and there were quite a few on her client list.

Left to her own devices, this talented woman could have been miserable and eventually left the firm to go and work elsewhere. But sitting next to her was another director who did like working for doctors, but had a list full of pharmacists. Two minutes' discussion, a flexible attitude to firm management and the problem was solved by resolving to swap clients.

The moral of this story is that your colleagues will have a different perspective to you, which means that a more satisfactory mix may be achieved just by moving clients around within the firm.

Once you have done the statistical analysis, then you can do the thinking! Which clients are the best fit? By 'fit', I mean which are the clients that best typify your firm's positioning? Which ones best suit your staff and their mix of skills? Which clients do you and your partners most like working on? These are the clients you want more of.

To get good answers to these questions you will need to work with your team. Everyone will have a different opinion and everyone should have input – there are no right or wrong answers. This is where the strength of the firm is really put to the test. If you are a new firm, just starting out, the questions are slightly different:

■ what drove you to start the firm in the first place?

■ what type of work or client are you passionate about?

■ in your previous jobs/firms, what has been the work you have most enjoyed; the clients you have most liked working for; the ones that have given you the most satisfaction?

The answers to these specific questions will enable you to balance the work across the firm. The trend of the answers will enable you to determine a path forward for the firm as a whole and target markets for each division.

Once you have drawn for yourself an idea of specific clients, try to work out what they have in common. What are the characteristics of these clients, what do they have in common in terms of:

■ location

■ size

■ industry

■ organisation type, and

■ work type?

These define your target market.

Finding the target market

Once you have found the common characteristics you can set about tracking down your target market.

Location

In many ways, this is one of the easiest ways to get started. Look at directories, join local clubs and talk to local chambers of commerce. Regional, state and council governments all have business offices dedicated to making business work in their area. Contacting them can give you access not only to lists but also other resources.

Becoming involved with these organisations can help you understand who is important and influential in the area, and can provide you with a great deal of practical and insightful advice.

Industry

Like local business development offices, industries have an interest in helping their constituents grow. In order to do this, they develop and run industry associations designed to help people within the industry, as well as helping people outside the industry to access and help people within the industry.

Becoming a member of an industry organisation, such as becoming involved with local chambers of commerce, provides you with information but also makes you part of the community. This helps give you credibility and access to target clients within that industry.

Organisation type

Organisations are in many ways organic – organisations of a similar type will have similar issues. Professional service firms, for example, have more similarities than they have differences. In many instances, organisations of the same type will be in the same industry (for example, lawyers will belong to the relevant law institute, and so on). In other instances, types of organisations are a bit more diverse: looking for 'medium-sized businesses in Melbourne involved in export' can be like trying to find a needle in a haystack.

YOU CANNOT FIND SOMETHING IF YOU'RE NOT LOOKING FOR IT

A FIRM was moving from smaller to larger clients. We identified the characteristics they were looking for, paid for some lists from Dun & Bradstreet and did as much desk research as we could to decide which would be the best targets.

In many instances, the type of organisations they wanted to work for were not known to them or their networks. The firm was faced with cold calls. As almost no-one likes cold calling and success rates can be low, I was not surprised when some partners made some calls but most did not. What the list of targets did though, was focus the mind on what we were looking for. Looking at those targets prompted other ideas and connections.

Interestingly, some four years later, the firm had proposed to or made contact with the majority of the organisations on the list, and was even working for some. Sometimes, just thinking in a straight line can help!

First, try looking at location and industry. Location can often be a good indicator of size – for example, businesses in a particular business park are likely to be of the same size. Industry can help to identify the relevant associations that may be able to assist. There may also be industry associations within industry associations that can help, such as lawyers in construction.

Finding information

All information sources cost money. Even when the hunting is done by your staff, there is still an opportunity cost for the time they spend not earning fees. Before you decide to spend time, effort and money pulling together information, it would be worthwhile considering how much effort and time will be required to do something about it.

You can waste a lot of time and effort pulling together target data that then sits gathering dust because you do not have time to do anything about it. You need time to pursue the information and turn information into opportunities, opportunities into reality and so on.

Do not collect more data than you can use. If you have decided that none of these definitions help and that you can get a return on investment from paying for a service, then the next step is to get help from information providers such as *Yellow Pages®*, *BRW*, *Dun & Bradstreet* and list brokers. Similarly, there are business development companies such as the Lead Generation Company that may be the best way of qualifying and finding a set number of leads that you can then pursue.

Whether you have a set number of named targets that you want principals to pursue, or whether you just nominate industries that you want to concentrate on, it is important to get firm-wide agreement and understanding of these targets and to be able to review progress against those goals.

WHAT TO DO NOW
- [ ] Review your client base.
- [ ] Define your target market.
- [ ] Assemble the information to help you find the target market.

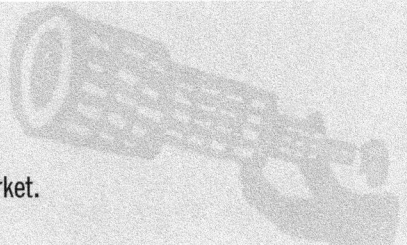

5 Looking outside – external analysis

No matter how well you do what you do, someone else is always competing for your clients. Know as much as possible about what you are up against.

Professional firms, on the whole, do not do much competitive analysis. It seems to be part of the mindset that sees the skills you have as unique, and is then able to rationalise the relative competitiveness of other firms. In every situation there is competition. Even if you cannot think of another firm which does exactly what you do, there will always be alternatives, and you need to weigh these up against what you have to offer the target audience.

Competing firms

This is the most obvious competition, a firm of the same type as yours – law, accounting, engineering, etc. Who are they, what do they offer, how many partners do they have and what do they specialise in? Websites are a good place to start, as is commercial information from your clients or colleagues who may have had some involvement with the competing firm.

When you are looking at industry associations, chambers of commerce or your professional magazines, look for the names of organisations offering the same services as you. Search online resources to see who is publishing papers, making presentations or running blogs in your area of expertise. Ask your friends, colleagues, clients and staff what they know about the firms concerned so you can start to build a picture of what you are up against. Keep this information together in a file so it can be easily updated on a regular basis. This is a good job for graduates to work on when they first start – it might look boring but it is a vital marketing tool and gives them a good view of the big picture.

When you have the raw data, try and add in the more qualitative information:
- what are their strengths/weaknesses?
- what are they known for?
- what is their reputation?
- how do their fees compare?

These are all important issues that will help you balance yourself against the competition and find your place in the market. You can find this information from surveys, benchmarks, media reports and most importantly, through word of mouth.

Other providers

In many areas, there will be more than one type of professional who can provide assistance. Bookkeepers can do financial accounts, some lawyers can do tax work, financial planners do estate planning. There are many areas where your main competitor may be a firm different to yours in structure or specialisation, but still capable of taking or keeping clients from you.

In many instances, these other providers may have a closer, more established relationship with the client than you do. Even if you have stronger technical skills, the depth of the relationship will always win out. The key here is not to try to displace the relationship, but to find ways of offering your skills to the client and allowing the existing relationship to continue.

Perhaps there are ways in which you and the competing provider can work together to your mutual satisfaction. If this is a new area for you (either geographically or just in experience terms), it is one that you need to master if you are going to grow your business effectively.

Doing it themselves

As with all the other options, in many instances clients can, or believe they can, do a great deal of the work themselves. They think this for a number of reasons:

- **They can**

    It is very easy to over-complicate the required activity and underestimate the skills of the client. Successful businesspeople achieve their position not just by being experts in their own field, but also by being able to learn new skills and find ways of getting things done. The instructions, templates and advice freely available can be excellent, and if a business is not too complicated it may be possible that the client can quite easily do things themselves. Auditing and surgery are probably the only skills without popular 'how-to' books, so there is always somewhere clients can turn for help to do things themselves!

- **They do not know the options**

    Business people run businesses, they do not spend their time looking at extra things they could be doing with the business other than making it run. As professionals, we should not assume that clients know what needs to be done and are ignoring it. Often the first step in a client relationship is identifying the issues. We need to make sure we bring important issues to their attention, through discussions, newsletters, seminars, websites and so on, so that they see the issues as well as the options for getting issues solved.

- **They think hiring help will be too expensive**

    When we have spent hours calculating our hourly rates and comparing them to competitors, determining profitability and being horrified yet again by the rising rates of professional salaries, it is difficult to believe that clients still think we are expensive.

In all of the interviews I have conducted with clients of professional service firms, they have almost never discussed fees in terms of being too expensive. The issue is not the amount of the fees, but the value they get for what they are paying.

The most critical work you can do on your professional service firm is to define the value that you bring to clients. You need to define the general value of your work but also more specifically the value to each client you work for. If a client does not see the value of hiring a professional it is because a professional has not shown them that value.

- **They do not do it at all**

  While it may seem to us, the seasoned professionals, that people cannot live without the services we offer, the truth is that they often can. With the exception of audit, much of the regular compliance work that needs to be done can be done with reference to the various government departments administering them. Although many of the non-compulsory elements may well be prudent, business owners may not see the need to get them resolved.

What to do?

In this type of situation, you can easily lose a potential client by badgering them over something they have decided they do not need. You have a number of options:

- stay doing work they know they do need until such time as they see the need for what you offer
- work on people within the business (say the bookkeeper, lawyer, accountant, etc) who do understand the need to have the issue dealt with
- where appropriate, find ways for the client to meet and mix with other clients for whom you perform the service and allow them to sell your skills for you, or
- retire gracefully – while tenacity is the hallmark of the good professional, knowing when to give up is also important.

LOOK AFTER TODAY, TOMORROW TAKES CARE OF ITSELF

I WORKED with a client who at more than 80 years of age did not have a set succession plan for his substantial business.

While we may regard this as foolhardy in the extreme, he simply explained that he had tried several succession plans over the past 20 years or so, but none had worked out.

He rationalised that while he was not immortal, he did not want to spend his last years of life looking over the horizon and planning his death. He reasoned, and quite rightly, that someone would work out what do with the business after he had gone. In the meantime, he was going to get on with running the business to make sure it was in as good a shape as possible. No matter that his professional advisers thought a plan was critical – it was not critical to him!

Over the horizon

You need to keep a weather eye on external macro issues affecting your business.

Technical issues

Every profession is beset by legislative change and its technical ramifications. You need to be sure you stay on top of these issues so you can help your clients when they are affected.

In some instances, for the extremely technically minded of you, this will mean keeping up-to-date, sitting on committees and staying at the forefront. For those of us with a more practical bent, it is probably easier to leave this to a technical service or to a professional association or network. Make sure you read the material sent out by these groups so you are at least aware of the issues that you need to be. Nominate someone in the firm as responsible for keeping an eye on these issues and bringing the whole firm up-to-date. Subscribing to international newsletters and/or technical services can also help you identify technical trends emerging overseas that may or may not affect your market.

Market issues

Competitors merging, arriving from overseas, having difficulties, industry groups forming or changing legislation; all these are issues affecting your marketplace that you need to be aware of. Set up Google Alerts on topics that you need to keep abreast of, visit the websites of competitors on a regular basis, encourage staff to keep an eye on what is happening in the marketplace. Include a discussion of changes in your marketplace in your regular team meetings so you can react as soon as something arises.

WHAT TO DO NOW
- [ ] Analyse the competition.
- [ ] Look over the horizon.
- [ ] Make sure you are well-informed.

6 Looking inside
— internal resources

Use the skills and experience of your staff as a business resource: identify who is good at what and develop the systems and processes to support them.

THE PRIMARY asset of any professional services firm lies in its staff and their knowledge, experience and skills. It is important then that you pay as much attention to these 'human resources' as you would to your physical resources. Make an objective assessment as to who has the best skills.

Business development skills

We all know people who are naturally good at attracting business. The truth is usually much more complicated, but trying to get such 'rainmakers' to deconstruct and understand, let alone explain, what they do is at best fruitless, at worst damaging.

> Think of business development like running. Almost all of us can do it, some much better than others. Some people love running, most people don't. But almost everyone can be taught to do it better, and even some people who hate it can learn to do it very well.

In order to maximise the value of their skills to the firm you need to find ways in which others can learn from rainmakers' skills:

- ensure when they see referrers they are accompanied by someone who can observe the way in which they interact, the questions they ask, the way they describe what they do;
- make sure contacts are kept in a central database where others can access them and information can be shared;
- have rainmakers mentor younger staff, providing them with tips, ideas and advice;
- do not have them conduct business development training. This may seem counter-intuitive, but as many of their skills will be innate, they will often be the worst teachers; but
- do have them review the content of the training that is proposed and, where possible, endorse it. This will legitimise the training in the eyes of the staff who admire them and reinforces that for most people, business development is a skill that can be learnt, rather than something you either have or do not have.

Networking

Often the person with the best business development skills and record is also the person with the best network. Sometimes, though, people have great networks but do not know how to use them. Look for people with connections to large, well-connected groups of people who belong to and attend clubs, associations, teams. Get them to think about who they know, who is connected to who.

This is often difficult to do in the abstract – it helps to have something specific to be looking for. So, when you are looking for a connection with a particular target, ask the network 'guru' if they know someone from the target's law firm, someone in the target's industry, someone who went to the target's school, someone who plays/supports sport with the target.

> It is a normal part of life that our networks get larger as we age – we simply know more people. Younger team members need to learn this early so they are conscious of who is in their networks, how the networks grow and where the connections are.

Get everyone in the firm to start thinking about who they know and who their network knows. Documented and managed, this is the beginnings of your firm's network. You will be surprised that by getting everyone's contacts into the one place you can start to build a sizeable firm network. The database that you keep this in needs to be easy to use, flexible and affordable.

A word about Customer Relationship Management systems

Customer relationship management (CRM) systems are like religions; everyone has a favourite, an opinion, an experience. There are even agnostics – those people who say there is no such thing as a good CRM system. As with most religious arguments, everyone is partly right. The following is my short, idiot's guide to CRM.

Invoices rule: the system you use to send out marketing and technical material should also generate the addresses for invoices. Invoicing has a way of focusing everyone's minds on what is important – if the address for the invoice is wrong, then everyone suffers. Invoices get followed up in a way that makes sure the database gets updated.

DIY: tempting though it might be to nominate a support person to be the database administrator, the responsibility for the sourcing and monitoring of the client data must lie with the principals who work with the clients. Support staff can do the actual system updating, but professional staff need to understand that the data is valuable and, most importantly, valuable to them.

Accessibility: all the information possible about the contact, target or client needs to be stored somewhere it is searchable and accessible. There is little point in a system where security and access are restricted, regardless of how 'pure' this keeps the data. Everyone needs to be able to hop in and out of the system to check on client information.

KISS: systems need to be simple enough for everyone to use. If systems are used only by support staff then the firm can be held hostage by staff holidays and absences. There will need to be someone within the firm who knows about the system's technical intricacies, but everyone needs to be able to read and access data.

Access: make sure that the data can be updated only by people who know the clients. Different levels of access can be complicated (and political) but essentially the professionals responsible for managing a client should be able to update the data. If someone else finds some information pertaining to that contact, then the main person responsible for that relationship needs to update the data.

GARBAGE IN, GARBAGE OUT

IF you don't care about the data you put into a system then you won't care about what comes out. No system delivers bad information: human intervention is needed for that. Keep track of the type of information you want from your CRM system regularly:

- names and addresses
- job titles
- relationship to the firm, and
- fees – current, ongoing, historical.

Then think harder:

- jobs referred to the firm
- football team
- memberships, and
- children.

Remember some of this information changes more often than others (spouses change more often than football teams). The list can go on and on, and the specifications for a system can get completely out of control.

Start with the simplest system that fits the criteria above, and make sure you are honest about when it needs to be replaced or upgraded.

Sustainability: the system needs to be supportable. Home-made systems (even self-tailored Lotus Notes or Excel) are great and do not require much out-of-pocket expenditure, but they can eat up internal staff resources. Off-the-shelf solutions always need tailoring and mean you are reliant on people outside the firm for support. The acid test is that you need to be able to run and maintain the system when the guru who designed it has left the firm, or the brilliant company that sold you the solution has gone out of business.

One size does not fit all: I have seen relatively large firms run very well on spreadsheets and small firms drown under the weight and cost of the most elaborate systems money could buy. You need to choose something manageable and affordable. You need to acknowledge when the system has outlived its usefulness and move on.

Systemise upkeep: even if you have a spreadsheet, make a time every week, month or at least year to review the data. *Do not do this at Christmas!* If you have not updated your data by November, send Christmas cards out to the database as it stands then use the returns to update the data. Apologise to or catch up with the people you did not send a card to. Too many cards are received late because people are updating their data. Better to get some addresses wrong than send all the cards out so late they arrive in the New Year!

Presentations

Like business development, there are people in the firm who are good at presenting, people who like presenting and people who need to present – and they are often not the same people. If you need someone to make presentations about the firm on a regular basis, then make sure it is someone who is good at presenting, is passionate about the firm and engages well with the audience.

You are better off having a single (over-used) spokesman than having people presenting who are either no good or do not care.

In many instances the best presenter will be the person who started the firm, or who has taken the firm to new areas. Their natural passion will communicate itself to an audience and it is often their presentation skills that are the reason many people joined the firm. The key is to find someone in each generation of the firm who has that skill.

This may not be the person who is the managing partner or director. This is not important. In many instances the skills required to run a firm and those required to present and enthuse do not exist in the same person. I have seen many firms work well where there is one principal (or even firm manager) who runs the practice and someone else who is the public face of the firm. Provided everyone understands the relative roles they play, this is a sensible use of skills and division of labour.

> Often the best words to describe your practice are those unrehearsed, heartfelt sentiments of the passionate enthusiast. When these words naturally pass from one generation to another within the firm, and change and adapt with the times, then you have the beginnings of a strong firm culture.

Again, as with business development, people who are naturally good often present without much preparation or assistance. The challenge then is that it is difficult for people to follow in their footsteps. If you have a natural presenter, videotape or at least record their presentations. This will allow you to review the presentations later and analyse what they said and how. This information can then be used to develop material and train others accordingly.

Written skills

Every professional thinks they are an excellent writer and most of them are wrong! If you can write so your audience understands, appreciates and knows how to act on your recommendations, then you are a good writer. In any practice there will be people who can write well and those who cannot. Most will be helped by standard letters and documents. The key is developing those and making sure people know how to use them.

For more persuasive forms of communications such as proposals and quotes, it is best to identify the person with the highest success rate (percentage of tenders/quotes won is a good place to start) and have a look at what they do. These documents can then be developed as a set of templates that other areas of the firm can adapt for their own purposes.

Do not be tempted, though, to let one person write all the firm's submissions. This develops a single point of failure and also means the person's personal style becomes the firm's style by default. Rather, encourage that person to delegate the task, preferably to a couple of people who can learn the required analysis, writing and presentation skills.

As with client information, be careful not to try to delegate too much of this task to support staff. Good support staff can be a fantastic help but it is tempting to let them run the process to the point where they develop the text. Everyone needs to start with an outline developed by the key principals in response to the particular client's needs. Text can then be added to the outline.

If you start with standard text, or use the last proposal as the template for the next one, then your proposals, presentation or technical papers will all start to sound the same and you run the risk of your professional staff not paying enough attention to the essence of the process – the client's business.

Technical specialisation

This may seem the most obvious of issues, but it is really important that you have a clear understanding of who has which technical skills. This is not just an issue of deciding who has the best tax skills but who is familiar with which industry, who has experience with which type of client.

The most obvious representation of this is the 'experienced hire', the professional who has joined your practice from industry, academia or another practice. The first thing we all pay attention to is the clients they have worked on and whether it is possible to attract some of them to our firm. But we need to look beyond the obvious and find out what type of people our staff have worked for, what value they provided and so on.

As part of induction make sure you work through the major client list with the new staff. Rather than just telling them about the client, ask them if they know anything about the client or the industry in which they operate. This needs to be done for *all* staff, professional or management.

The key, then, is to make sure you know as much about your staff as possible. Every member of staff should have a CV, but more importantly they need to have a document somewhere on the system from which that CV is drawn. In a perfect world, client names and jobs would be added to the document every time work was completed. Inputs to the list of who has which technical skill (which can be as simple as a spreadsheet) need to come from:

- work completed for the firm
- work completed outside the firm
- academic experience
- voluntary experience – staff may have done relevant work for not-for-profits, and
- staff reviews – it is important staff at all levels are given the chance where possible to work on the type of work that attracts them and that interests them.

Skills development

Gap analysis

So we know what type of work we want to do and clients we want to work for, and the position we want to occupy in the market. Now we need to work out whether we have the skills, tools and team we need to get there. Get the person responsible for each specialisation to detail the skill set they believe the team needs to have in order to be able to offer the service. This then becomes the start of a skills matrix (see Table 7).

TABLE 7: SKILLS MATRIX							
				Skill			
Industry	Audit	Accounting	Corporate advisory	Presenting	Tenders	Networking
Engineering						
Food and beverage						
Financial services						
Manufacturing						
Not-for-profit						
Retail						
IT and T						
Timber						

Each professional should complete a table for themselves when they join the firm, and summarise their experience into each part of the table. These tables are then collated and we can insert the names of the professionals who have skills in that industry. While this may seem difficult to do, the real pain is in getting everyone to complete the information in the first place. This information enables you to pitch with the confidence that you have the skills available to do the job.

Filling the gaps

Apart from being a useful tool for personal and team development, the skills matrix is an invaluable tool in recruitment. If everyone in the firm has the same idea of the type of skills the firm needs, then they can be on the lookout for people that have those skills or experience.

KNOW WHAT SKILLS YOU HAVE – AT ALL LEVELS

AN RFT came in from a large retailer. The firm had the technical skills to do the work but was short on retail experience.

When the tender was put together, CVs for the partners and managers proposed for the job were pulled together and edited to emphasise the retail experience they had. A team was chosen based on the people available.

When the firm failed to win the work I rang the retailer to ask for a debrief on why we had not won it. They told me they had wanted to see the experience that all the team had, right down to the lowest levels. They said in their experience, most younger staff had had more retail working experience than older team members and even though it might have been in part-time jobs, they wanted to select a firm whose team members would best understand them and their businesses.

Needless to say, the junior members of the proposed team had worked in retail during university, and one of them had worked for the retailer concerned. We were too busy worrying about the technical skills required to look at industry experience of the more junior team members. It is not just that we did not mention this experience in our tender, we did not know, we did not ask!

Training

Training is not just about ensuring people stay up-to-date, it is also about ensuring people stay. Training is one of the key elements in any staff retention strategy. Consider including the skills matrix in Table 7 in your standard review process. Each staff member then completes the skills matrix at review time.

This helps keep the information up-to-date, but importantly it shows both the staff member, and the person they report to, the progress they have made throughout the year. This makes them not only feel good about their achievements but also see the work they have done in terms of their own personal development.

The information in this matrix can be used to:

- update corporate marketing material
- update capability statements
- update CVs
- provide information for tenders, and
- develop training schedules.

At their review, each staff member should be encouraged to discuss not just which skills they wish to use but also which industries they would like to work in. Training can then be planned and developed according to these lists. While it may appear that for a small (or perhaps even a large) firm this will result in a huge and impossibly varied list of training that is required, this training does not need to be developed or delivered in-house. There is good professional training available on-site, off-site and online for all the skills a professional firm needs.

Start with your professional association and then look to the relevant industry associations to see what is available for you and your team.

AN ANSWER TO THE QUESTION THAT WASN'T ASKED

A PROMISING senior associate turned down a chance to become a partner in a city legal firm in favour of becoming a partner in a smaller legal practice in a regional centre.

At his exit interview (had he had one), the firm would have discovered it was not that he was looking to return to the country (although that was a factor) but that he had wound up working in an area of the practice he had no interest in.

He had been promoted and rewarded for excellent work, but at no point in the review process had anyone asked him what type of work he wanted to do, or what type of client he wanted to work with.

The one that got away!

Practising

With both technical and marketing skills, you need practice to keep these skills relevant and up-to-date. What we tend to do, however, is have lots of time for practising and updating technical skills but not business development skills. There are a number of ways in which team members can practise their skills:

- encourage them to get involved in community activities where they can practise talking about themselves and what they do
- ask staff to present to potential and new recruits about the firm
- hold nights when their peers from other professional firms can get together and practise talking about what they do
- get staff to meet with the firm's best referrers and test their presentation skills on them, and
- take staff along whenever principals meet with clients, so they can see how it is done and develop the confidence to talk to clients themselves.

WHAT TO DO NOW

- ☐ Know your firm's skill sets.
- ☐ Identify networks.
- ☐ Implement CRM.
- ☐ Develop presentation skills.
- ☐ Harness written skills.
- ☐ Understand and nurture technical specialisations.
- ☐ Do gap analysis.
- ☐ Train and practise.

7 Brand and positioning

The secret weapon for services is trust; brands are critical, because they help services overcome the challenge of being something you can't touch or see.

THE NEXT step is to position the organisation and the services it supplies in relation to your competition. Positioning is concerned with identifying, developing and communicating what makes your organisation's services superior to those of your competitors.

Customers buy according to the total value of a service. For a client to want to buy your services, we need to look at:

- what we can provide them with
- the total value (service, product, people, image) of the service to the customer, less
- the total cost (money, time, people, energy).

Each service, therefore, relies on our ability to determine the total cost of the product, then the parts of the service that are value-added and those that represent real value to the client.

A bit of theory

There are four major things that set services apart from products (that is, why you can't sell services like you sell washing powder).

Services are:

Intangible: you cannot see or touch them.

Variable: every service is different every time, because they are ...

Inseparable: you cannot separate the service from the people delivering *or* receiving it: in each instance, the fact that people are so closely involved means there are subtle differences of delivery and experience.

Perishable: services have to be delivered in real time and cannot be stored for future use.

These differences present challenges (see Table 8) to all aspects of the service firm's management – operations, finance and marketing. Logistically, the firm must resolve the issues concerned with the customer's involvement, people as part of the product, quality control, delivery in real time and different distribution channels. Both finance and operations have to ride the challenges presented by perishability. While also involved to some extent in all of these issues, marketing's greatest challenge is to overcome intangibility.

TABLE 8: MEETING THE SERVICES CHALLENGE		
Characteristic	**Solutions**	
Intangibility	■ strong branding ■ presence of offices, uniforms and signage	■ testimonials ■ case studies
Variability	■ standards ■ processes, methodologies	■ quality control processes ■ training, mentoring
Inseparability	■ choose staff wisely ■ choose clients carefully	■ manage interactions between staff and clients ■ staff retention policies
Perishability	■ document processes	■ schedule work throughout the year

The secret weapon for services is trust. The level of trust differs with each service as the involvement of the customer alters. Customers must trust that their accounts are prepared correctly, their contracts have been thoroughly checked and their drawings reviewed.

Once the service starts being delivered, if there is close contact between the customer and the provider (for example in a court case) then the need for absolute trust dissipates. When there is less contact, (for example when you are liaising with the authorities on a client's behalf) then the need for trust is constant, because they cannot touch or see the service being delivered. It is here that brands become critical to services, as they help make the service more tangible.

In positioning your service, you should also consider where your industry, organisation, product line and service are currently positioned, and what change you are seeking to make.

What is our brand?

'Brand' refers not just to the name of the firm but also to the design and all the physical representations of the firm. This will include the obvious things like stationery, as well as less obvious elements like fit-out of the office. A standard list would include:

- stationery (letterhead, with compliments slips, envelopes, business cards, memo, fax, templates)
- internal and external forms (bills/invoices, cheques)
- signage (reception signs, external and internal signs)
- advertising (directories/display/non-display/cooperative)
- sponsorships
- publications (client, staff, manuals)
- templates

- ID passes
- promotional items
- websites (internet, intranet)
- direct marketing and direct mail
- trademarks, and
- presentation materials.

The key is to look at all of the brand elements such as name, colour, typography, image, etc that are used on each of these items and review them critically, as described below.

There is a great deal of discussion and literature about brand. Most of this is too theoretical to need to bother with for your professional practice. In layman's terms the key issues are:

- what do you call yourself?
- how are you represented?
- what does your name say about you?
- should/could you consider changing it to make it more relevant?

The best place to start with brands is where did it come from? Sometimes the heritage of the brand can be important, and of value to both recruits and clients alike. For example, were the original founders of the firm respected experts in their field, have their names become synonymous with the area of specialisation or were they seen to be pioneers in their field? If so, maybe keeping their names is a good idea. Brands should:

Reveal the product: difficult to avoid with professional services – potential clients need to know what you do. In these days of web-driven information gathering, do not underestimate the importance of having your name say what you do. Be careful, though, that the brand does not restrict the scope of the work you can reasonably expect to do in the future. Don't call yourself Commercial Architects if you think you may build houses later on.

WHAT'S IN A NAME?

WHAT we call ourselves as an organisation affects the way that our customers see us. Giving a name to our organisation gives us a valuable opportunity to create a positive image in the minds of our customers.

As a service provider, a name is even more critical, because as we have discussed, it renders the service tangible.

Many professional practices name themselves after the people who started the firm, full names, initials and so on. Certainly when you start a firm, if your principals have strong reputations then it may be a good tactic to emphasise their role in the new venture. At other times, though, you may want to consider some other issues:

- what will happen if you want to sell the firm?
- will the name of the firm improve or reduce the value of the firm to potential buyers?
- what if other principals buy into or take over management of the firm?

If these outcomes are likely, probable or even just possible, then it might be more sensible to find or develop a name that is not related to the principals of the firm.

Identify a target customer: if you have a particular type of target customer in mind, then a reference to that in your name can help, for example Corporate Solutions is clearly focused on corporate businesses.

Promote positive perception: this sounds obvious, and if the names of the principals promote a positive perception because of their reputations, then that will do. If, however, you are starting out, then a brand that makes people think positively about your firm is important.

Values

Have a look back at the values you decided on for the firm. Does the brand reinforce, contradict or have nothing to do with the values? Chosen and expressed correctly, values should not change through the life of an organisation. From time to time though, the ways a brand looks can be dated and need refreshing. Whenever you change or update your brand, you need to make sure it is still an accurate reflection of the values.

Do we need to do anything to change our brand?

If the answers to these questions reveal a gap between what you want the firm to stand for and what it does stand for, then you need to weigh up whether and how the brand needs to change to better reflect the desired positioning. If you decide you need to change the firm's brand, define the gap and then call in neutral professionals to help. It will save you time and grief in the long term.

Keeping it unemotional

The challenge with brands is that they are, by definition, emotional. The whole idea behind the Coke brand, for example, is that the marketers of Coke want you to be emotionally attached to their cola rather than the competition. Whether there is any real difference between the products is irrelevant – the key is to establish a different emotional relationship between the customer and the service. The same is true of all brands, and the

---

Before you choose a name, also consider:

- what does it mean to the target market? It is all too easy to determine what the brand means to you as the business's owners. After all, it may be your names or a name that you thought of. But more importantly, what does it mean to your clients and staff, both existing and potential?
- that the name does not mean anything rude in any of the languages you think you might trade in (test Spanish and Chinese as a minimum. On a web-based translator, take the English word and translate it and then translate it back – this is a rough but effective test).
- availability of domain names on the internet (www.melbourneit.com.au).
- availability of the business and trading name (www.asic.gov.au).
- availability of any future trademarks (www.ipaustralia.gov.au).

ones we are most emotional about are our own brands. Think of your name, and whether you like to be called by one version of it or another: this is probably something you feel strongly about. The same is true for the firm's brand and is further complicated in professional services by the number of people who 'own' the brand.

So how do you make decisions about the brand without everyone getting too emotional about it?

> There is no easy way to test whether values and brand align other than to literally look at them next to each other. When you look at the brand and the values next to each other, do they look consistent? Would someone who had never seen the brand before find it a good fit or incongruous with the values?

Ask the stakeholders

Pull together a group of people, some business owners, some employees, possibly even some clients if you know them well enough and think they would like to get involved. Get someone independent (or a professional facilitator if you get stuck) to run a session with these stakeholders and hear from them:

- what they think of the brand
- what they think the brand means
- what they thought of the brand when they first came across it
- whether their view has changed
- if so, why?
- whether they think the brand will serve the firm into the next decade, and
- if not, which elements will not and why?

It is important in all of this to remember this is not a popularity contest – you need to come up with a view of the brand that will grow with the firm into the future, not just something you like.

Back to design

Once you have decided to launch the brand or change it, do not decide what it should look like. Use the positioning, values and gap analysis to form the basis of a brief for a design company.

Design is emotional and best left in the hands of professionals who sit at some distance from the brand. Let them determine how the physical representation of the brand needs to change. Ask for a quote and make sure the quote includes at least two, and no more than four, designs to choose from. Put these designs back to the brand review group and let that group make the decision about which design best represents the firm. Again, choose something that will work, not just something you like.

Messages

How do you describe the firm when someone asks?

This is both a big-picture question and a practical issue. Think out loud about how you answer this type of question. Try not to re-engineer it as you go – just put down what it is you normally say when asked. Do you describe the firm based on size, location, client type, skill set, specialisation? For example: 'We are a small suburban accounting firm.'

What you say reveals a lot about you and your firm and will obviously affect the view of the listener. 'We' suggests there is more than one principal, 'small' will depend on the listener's view, and understanding, of the market. If they are from a regional area themselves then they may think this means you are a sole practitioner. If they are from the city, they may infer you have fewer than 50 staff.

Using your location may be an attractive thing to a potential client from your area, but it also may make a city dweller think you have little to offer, even if you specialise in their industry and are able to use technology and communications to service them regardless of location. 'We are a suburban accounting firm', is a very different message from 'We are a corporate accounting firm based in the suburbs', and yet they could both describe the same firm.

What do clients say?

If you cannot arrive at any sensible description of the firm among yourselves, then consider asking some of your best clients and see what they say. Clients will often deliver a completely different idea of what they think you do than you would yourselves.

The important thing about what clients say is that, assuming the feedback is positive, what they have to say about you will usually also be what would attract other clients like them to the firm.

Finding out what clients think reminds you what you need to do to keep clients happy. Treat this as you would a health check – find out every year, whether you like it or not! This is vital information you need if your firm is not just to survive but to prosper.

It is not that your clients' view of what you do should override your own, but you need to consider how hard it is to change an opinion once it is formed. If your good clients (that is, the type of clients you want more of) describe you as a small suburban firm, you will not be able to convince them, regardless of how hard you try, that you are a specialist corporate firm. For this reason, it is important to check your goals against what your clients say about you, so you can determine how realistic your goals are and to make sure you do not disenfranchise current clients while trying to attract new ones.

What do staff say?

Another good test is what your staff say about the firm. With recruitment being one of the major issues facing professional services firms worldwide, it is as important to market to recruits as it is to market to clients and potential clients. Knowing what your staff think of the firm and what attracted them to work with you is critical information in determining how you describe the firm.

Pull these lists of words and descriptions together into one list, edit them to remove duplication and make sure you are saying something about your firm that is:

- true (demonstrable now and maintainable in the future)
- distinctive from your competition
- easy to understand, and
- short and to the point.

These words may be your values, your mission, vision or whatever other words you have developed to describe the firm. Once developed, these messages can be used to form the basis of your firm's marketing tools.

WHAT TO DO NOW

☐ Think about your firm's name and design.
☐ Ask your stakeholders.
☐ Develop meaningful messages.

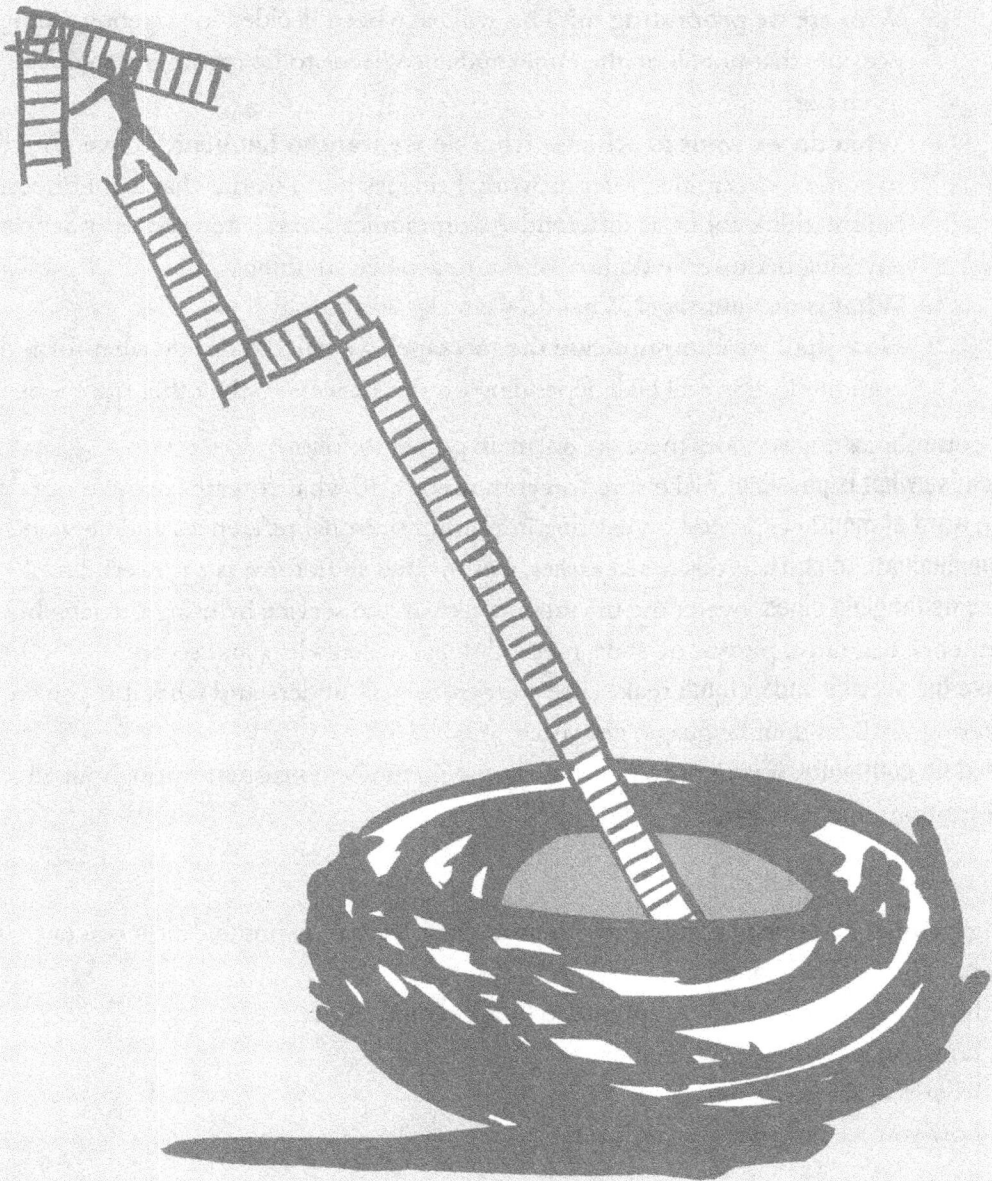

The first communications you have with potential clients are critical: make sure they clearly represent the values and 'personality' of your firm.

THE DECISION is often made to communicate ('we need a brochure') before we know what we are communicating. Before you leap to put words to paper, stop and think.

The questions to be answered are fairly simple.

- **Who are we promoting to?** This will have been decided in targeting, but it is possible that not all of the target audience needs to be communicated with at any given time.
- **What do we want to achieve, what do we want to happen?** Do we want them to come to a seminar, refer us work, bring issues to us they have not discussed before, think about us differently? Communication is often seen as not achieving anything because we do not set out to achieve anything!
- **What is our message?** What do we really want to say?
- **How shall we communicate the message?** We need to decide what form the communication will take depending on the answers to the other questions.

In communicating services there are six main points to follow:

Promise what is possible: make sure you commit only to what you are sure you can deliver

Use word of mouth: capitalise on existing important personal references and networks

Communicate to staff: as discussed earlier, a motivated staff force is a powerful tool

Provide tangible clues: overcome the intangibility of the service by using the tangible elements, diagrams, photos of staff, methodologies, clients lists and so on

Make the service understood: make sure your customers understand what it is you are offering – talk in their language, not yours, and

Maintain continuity: it is important the image or theme be consistent throughout all promotions and over time.

Engagement and retainer letters

Engagement and retainer letters are often the first formal communication you have with a client. They should contain:

- how pleased you are to be appointed/reappointed
- how you want to work together
- what you are going to deliver
- how you are going to deliver it

- the frequency and method of communication
- what they need to do so you can deliver your services
- how often you are going to invoice
- the level of detail to be contained in those invoices, and
- the schedule of fees that will be applied.

At this point we also need to communicate:

- what we are not going to deliver, and
- how the relationship will be managed if something goes wrong.

At this point many of you will be saying, 'Yes, that's all very well, but the lawyers, etc'. I am not naïve enough to imagine that these letters are not important legal documents, or that we do not need to protect ourselves from potential litigation – my point is that if this is your first formal communication with the client then you should start as you mean to proceed. The letter should be a communication first and a legal document second.

Take legal advice by all means, but see if you cannot have the legal issues and obligations contained either in a comprehensive terms-and-conditions section or even perhaps in a separate contract. All too often first letters spend more time saying what we will *not* do rather than focusing on what we *will* do. Find a way to make sure the letter communicates the personality of your firm and the enthusiasm with which you are embarking on this new relationship.

Standard letters

Like engagement letters, standard letters should communicate the firm's values and the ways in which it would like to be seen to communicate. Think back to the 'personality' of the firm – this is a useful tool for determining the tone that standard letters should take.

Make sure your letters are:

Easy to understand: remember that many of the standard letters you send will not be read by people with the same level of education (or degree of interest) that you have. If you find it difficult to write to this level, then hire someone to write some letters for you or take your standard letters and test them on a person from outside the firm. Use this feedback to review the content of all your letters.

> If you are a firm for whom formality is part of your personality, then be formal by all means. But all too often firms decide to have a more relaxed approach to working with clients and yet their letters remain stiff and formal. Try reading the letters out loud. If they sound pretentious, then perhaps you have taken the formality too far.

Short: a short letter is much more likely to be read, understood and acted on than a long letter. Look carefully at what you are expecting the letter to contain and see if there is any content that would be better in a contract, terms and conditions document or other separate communication.

Only templates: standard letters should make life easier, but they cannot do all the work. Make sure everyone knows that standard letters are there as templates and are not an excuse for not thinking about what you want to say. Really, the principal responsible for the relationship with the client should at least read over every letter sent to the client, if only for legal reasons.

Flexible: make sure the letters can be adjusted to say what you want them to say. It is better to have a few flexible standard letters than to have one for every occasion. If you have too many letters then it makes it difficult to find the right one and also impossible to maintain if ever any of your firm's details change (such as your address).

Invoices

Value

Clients do not talk about price or fees as much as they talk about value. Invoices, on the other hand, usually talk only about fees. It is not uncommon for clients to have very little formal communication other than invoices. Some firms use the invoice as a simple request for payment, others use them as an opportunity to deliver a monthly progress report to the client. In either instance, the important thing to remember is that invoices are communications between you and the client. To this end, they need to communicate:

- what was done
- the value this represents to the client
- under whose instruction the work was done
- who did it, and
- under which payment agreement (quote, contract, etc).

Pricing

Separate but related to value is the issue of price. Price is critical in determining the value the customer receives. At a regular point each year you will need to look at the price you are going to charge for the services you provide. Pricing decisions need to take into consideration:

- cost – to you and the client;
- positioning – the customer's perception of the product;
- the customer's ability to pay;
- the value of the service to the customer;
- competitive prices;
- service capacity;
- the level and nature of demand; and
- the potential future of the work and the client.

There are many consultants who are experts on fee-setting, and I will defer to their greater knowledge and experience. But once you have set the fee structure, consider the following issues:

- tempting though it may be to discount current work against future work, the old 'bird in the hand' adage still stands
- there will be instances when a particular client and/or job would seem to require different fee arrangements. Be careful not to start providing discounts or differential fees on a regular basis because clients will find out from others they are on different arrangements
- have a process for reviewing fees every year and include a standard increase in fees driven by CPI or some similar measure, and
- never be embarrassed by what you charge – it is in the end a real reflection of what you are worth.

Publications

This is the most visible part of the marketing mix and therefore the one that many people concentrate on first rather than making the important decisions that drive promotion. The key to any communications program is that it needs to be:

Relevant: it needs to include the type of communications that your clients and target clients want to receive. It needs to be only as sophisticated as your clients need it to be. Publish only if it is worthwhile and keep the content as simple as possible.

Sustainable: once you start communicating you create expectations that you then need to meet. This means you need to establish a realistic publication schedule – develop a piece of communication first and keep track of how long it takes to pull it together (both real and elapsed time) before you commit to the frequency of the publication. Nominate someone to be responsible for the publication and make sure they have the time and interest to commit to getting the communication out on a regular basis.

Efficient: this does not mean getting it done as quickly as possible, it means reduce, reuse, recycle to make the most of the content your firm is already producing. It also means making sure as many people as possible who might be interested get to hear, read or see your material.

Websites

Like it or not, websites are practically compulsory. The first thing most potential clients – and certainly all recruits – will do when referred to you is to look at your website and find out about you. You need a website and you need to keep it up-to-date. If you do not have a website, consider one of the domain and hosting packages available from reputable suppliers that offer a package deal (such as Melbourne IT, eKnowhow, etc). Following their instructions to get the site started is relatively simple, but make sure you diarise to spend a few hours looking at it every month and considering what you could do to make it better.

If your staff look at your website and you don't, then you will quickly become out of touch with what is happening. Things you may want to think about include:

Budget

Despite, or perhaps because of, the need to regularly update websites they can be very expensive. You can spend as much money as you have on a website and not be any further advanced. If the cost of managed sites is too high, then look at getting one of your own staff to build and update the site. They probably know how to do it already, but if not, then there are some good packages and training programs out there that could be a better investment than paying an agency.

Ease of management

Sites need to be easily changeable. This means you need to be able to do this work in-house. You do not need to be web designers but you do need someone who can make changes to text and load new images. If you are paying someone externally to develop the site then make sure you can use the content management system to update the site. This is the system you use to change the text – you do not need to be able to do it yourself, but if it looks so complicated that you cannot even understand it, then it is probably too hard.

Review website content and 'look and feel'

The way a website works and feels needs to reflect the personality of the practice. While the words can be written to include the values, it is important that the imagery and navigation also reflect the way the practice feels. When potential clients, and especially recruits, enter your website they should feel as if they are looking into a window of your office. When they come to see you, your firm should be familiar to them.

Identify performance/ efficiency improvement

There are a number of analytical packages (such as Google Analytics, AW Stats, etc) that can provide easy-to-understand statistics that allow you to measure the performance of your website. Whoever builds your website should be able to set up the package for you free of charge. Get them to show you how the packages work and what information they can provide. Once you get your head around the stats and what you need to measure, then it is a matter of reviewing these on a regular basis.

Ensure unique content and regular updates

Much of your success in being found by search engines relies on the frequency with which you update your website. This does not mean you need to change all the text every month, but it does mean that you need to add new events, publications and other material to ensure your site is constantly offering something new.

Review keywords

Keywords are those words that people will use to search for your site. You need to decide which words you think people would use, test them with your analytics packages on the website and then by searching on those keywords yourself, and seeing the sort of sites that come up in response. Your web developer should be able to give you some more detailed processes that will help you determine a list of keywords for your website. Once you have this list, use it to make sure those words are included in as many of the pages of your website as possible. Although it is important to use these words, be careful that you do not torture the language to the point where it is incomprehensible.

Check Google rankings

Check these once a month and use them as a tool for reviewing the success of your web management. You should be able to improve your Google ranking until it at least reflects your market position relative to your competitors.

Listings in online directories

As the number of offline directories diminishes, it becomes important to have your firm listed in online directories. Certainly make sure your *Yellow Pages*® or the equivalent directory listing is up-to-date. This way, if all else fails people will be able to find you. Be careful, though, that you do not waste money on being listed in directories that are not at least higher ranking in search engines such as Google than your firm is itself. Many directories

DOES IT PAY TO ADVERTISE?

THERE seem to be two schools of thought about advertising for professional firms — it works or it does not.

The first school thinks (perhaps hopes) that an ad will solve the firm's issues and bring in clients that do not seem to come any other way. The second school is the doubters, many of them old enough to remember when a shingle in the high street was all that was allowed. Many decades later, it seems many professionals see this as still the rule. While the actual restrictions have long been lifted, there is still a lingering distaste about advertising. The truth is, though, regardless of whether we like it or not, professionals provide a service and charge fees accordingly. Take-up of your service depends on many factors and while those against advertising are right in assuming that advertising alone will not bring clients to the firm, it does have a part to play.

Before you decide to advertise, consider the points made regarding all promotions above and decide:

- who is going to see the ad – unless a reasonable number of the people seeing the ad are targets, referrers or influencers then it is a waste of time. Look at professional journals, publications that appeal to the target organisation, location or other characteristics to ensure it is targeted;
- what you are going to say – ads do not have much time to communicate. The most effective ads are those that remind the customer about the brand. They will still need to hear about you from somewhere else, but ads can effectively position you when they do; and
- what you can afford – compared to other forms of promotion, advertising is expensive and relies on repetition, so it is not for the faint-hearted. If you only have enough money to run a small campaign, consider spending your money on direct mail, PR or other more cost-effective options instead.

promise brilliant rankings and ploys to attract potential targets but they are little more than lists of names with nothing to recommend them.

Email lists/eNewsletters

If you consider the fees generated from clients as the major asset of your firm, then the names and addresses of the people who pay those fees is also valuable. We have talked about CRM systems elsewhere and at the risk of it sounding like a rant, it is vitally important that you keep your databases up-to-date and have a system for checking them. Whether this means you get a data house to run your data against online directories, or making sure every time your staff make a call they call from the database to check the phone numbers, you need a system.

Make sure you keep track of how people come to your firm. Even if this is only a list in your head, or a checklist somewhere in the system, it is vital to know how people find you and what they are looking for when they do. I know, for example, that every year I earn enough money from contacts generated through Christmas cards and from new people coming through the *Yellow Pages*® to justify paying for both. It is for this reason that we ask about this in our client service interviews – often the principal concerned has forgotten or 'remembered' the wrong information about how clients came to the firm. You need to really *know* what works.

Newsletters, like all other forms of communication, should be sent out only when you have something to say and an audience which wants to hear it. This means you need to know which clients want to know what. eNewsletters have a number of advantages here as people can opt out themselves and you can tell how many people read it, how soon after you send it, etc. The challenge, though, is that as email traffic increases it becomes less likely your newsletter will get read at all.

Check with clients on a regular basis how they want to receive information (hard copy, soft copy, email summary, podcast, etc). If they want a hard copy, see if you can find a way for them to receive it from your staff by hand, either at a meeting, office visit or even third-party event. In this way it may avoid being thrown out with all the other unsolicited mail.

Blogs

Blogs are a popular way to communicate (especially with with people under 35) and can be very useful for recruitment. Be careful, though, that your blogs are written by people who care about what they write and about you as a firm and that you have some right of reply. There are many articles (and blogs!) about blogging – make sure you have some idea about how they operate before you sanction one from your firm. In short, they must not be advertorial – they need to be genuine user-driven content.

Technical papers/research

Once you have decided on the areas of technical expertise you want your firm to be known for, and which principals will be responsible for which technical specialisation, it is a question of deciding how you promote that technical skill. While most of your targets and clients will not necessarily be interested in the full technical detail, if you want to gain credibility in that field you will need to put some effort into publishing technical papers.

The form these papers take will differ depending on your profession and the technical specialisation, but the steps for getting them done will be the same.

Contact the relevant professional or industry organisation, look at their website, read their magazine or newsletter. Before you have someone start writing, spend some time looking at the topics of the most recent articles. Which topics of interest have not been covered, which topics recur? Develop a list of topics and then contact the organisation to discuss the idea of an article, what their deadlines are, what their specifications are and so on. The specifications will tell you how they will receive technical papers, how long they should be, whether you need a summary, file formats, etc. Follow these specifications as if they were the instructions for writing an essay at university – otherwise your efforts may be wasted.

Once you have a technical article written, publish it on your own website and send links to clients or contacts who might be interested. Consider other ways in which the content could be reused in magazines, websites, online article directories, etc.

Things to remember for all forms of marketing communication:
- think about the audience, who are they, what they want to know, what type of language they are used to
- spell-check
- get someone who has not seen the material before to read it and check the content makes sense
- find someone who is a formatting bully to check the punctuation and formatting
- put the name of the author, the copyright symbol and the date in the footer
- make sure you include page numbers and references where appropriate
- name it according to its content and audience and file it where it can be found again, and
- think about where you can reuse that material – industry publications, press releases, sending it to clients who might be particularly interested, on your website, sending it to other relevant websites, posting some of it to relevant blogs.

Proposals

There will be some areas of work that will always require the drafting and submitting of tenders, expressions of interest or proposals. Proposals can be critical, especially when you are building competency in a new field or area of practice. If you have to start from scratch and get your name known in the right circles, there can be worse ways than submitting tenders to the organisations of interest, particularly if you get to present your credentials in person.

Once you have moved past this phase, then you need to decide how much time and effort you want to spend on proposals. Effort needs to be balanced with the chances of success – for example, you may decide not to submit if you will not have a chance to present your team in person.

The key is to develop a process that helps you understand why you are doing this work and what your expectations are. One of the most critical issues with tenders is to record the amount of time you spend on them. By recording the time your professional and support staff spend on proposals you can review your commitment and gain some idea of the return you are getting on your investment.

The main reason for lack of success in proposals is not having enough information in the first place. The list of questions below is not exhaustive and should be tailored to suit your circumstances. Whether you ask these questions directly of the client or find out the answers yourself, the key is to make informed decisions and not blindly tender at every opportunity.

Proposal process

Keep track: when the opportunity to bid comes in, register how it came in (formal/informal, expression of interest, request for tender, referral, existing contacts, prospects, etc), when it is due and what the final result is. This way over the long run you can track what work you get from where.

Find a champion: as with almost everything else in a professional services firm, you need to have a principal who is both *keen* and *available* to drive the proposal process or it will not happen. They do not need to do the work, but they need to take responsibility for getting it done. It is important that everyone on the team is involved in all the decisions rather than just being told what to do. This is not about consensus, this is about consultation.

Treat them as a client from the start: meet the client at their site and get answers to as many questions as possible. What does the client want, how and why? How will they choose? Make sure you know as much about the client as you can.

Treat it as business from the start: have a clear view of whether you want this work or not and why. Develop a pricing model to assess price and profitability. Review whether you have a conflict, and if you have the resources that will be needed before you start.

Be realistic: Consider the competitive (can we beat the competition?) and risk (is there any risk to our business or reputation?) issues. Identify where you can seriously add value and if you cannot, then consider saying no.

Plan it like a project: start back from the due date and make sure you have allowed yourself enough time to write, edit, print, collate and bind the final draft (sounds obvious, but the end is the most common place people run out of time).

Don't start from scratch: get your marketing team or someone else with good knowledge of the systems and files to find, review and edit case studies and CVs. Put all the available information into a proposal template and see what is missing.

Get a reviewer: the manager responsible for the job can review previous jobs and assess relevant fees, issues write-offs and propose relevant fee structure/price/budget. Ask an independent principal/manager (someone from a different division or who has not been involved in the bid so far) to review and comment on the draft, including the pricing elements. Review the draft against client requirements and strategy. Edit and spell-check.

Show enthusiasm: proposals can often be very dry things and you may not have room to communicate your enthusiasm. Use the covering letter to make it clear how much you want the work.

Deliver it right: check and recheck all the specifications and detail about the delivery – do not leave this to someone else. If everyone checks it then hopefully nothing will go wrong.

Present well: look at the presentation as the real reason you did the proposal. If you get to present then at least your time has been well spent – you will have the chance to demonstrate your knowledge and team in person. Confirm presentation format, style and length, members of the client interview panel and the likely area of focus. Decide the role of individual team members and practise – do a run-through with someone playing the role of the client asking questions.

Follow-up: if advised that you are unsuccessful, phone or write to the client thanking them for the opportunity and requesting feedback. Look at this as an opportunity to offer other services to the client. If you really want to work for the client, keep them on your database – you never know. Even if you win, ask why – you might learn something. And finally, don't forget to thank the referrer or source.

> Conducting a routine debrief for a proposal we had not won, I asked the client why the successful firm had won. They told me that the firm had put a proposal to them years ago and had since kept in touch with both paper and personal communication. The client felt that all the tenderers had the skills but that the winning team was obviously keen. Persistence can win the day.

Events

Events hold a fraught position in most professionals' lives. We know they are important and valuable ways of imparting or learning information and of networking with clients or potential clients and referrers. On the other hand, they chew up out-of-hours time and can seem to be a waste of effort. As with all forms of marketing communication, it is important to work out what you are doing and why.

Holding events

Holding events can be time-consuming and if you are not careful, expensive. Hold events only if:

- you genuinely have a reason for doing so – that is, you have a topic that you are experts in or you have found an expert who can talk on a topic for you.
- you have people who really want to hear what you have to say. Make sure you are only inviting clients, targets or referrers to whom the topic will be of interest and avoid having the same people come to everything. If you are having trouble getting enough people to attend, consider asking colleagues in related fields, such as accountants, lawyers, bankers or advisers, to come and perhaps even share hosting of the event with you.

- you have a passion for doing it. There is nothing worse than going to an event that you are not entirely sure you want to go to and finding that the people from the firm holding it do not know why they are there either.
- you have time. You will need enough time to develop the topic, enough lead time to send out and follow up the invitations and then enough time for your team to attend on the day. You will also need to follow attendees up afterwards by sending them a copy of the presentation or asking for feedback at the end of the session.
- you have facilities – you need to have enough room to host enough guests as well as the number of your own professionals that you need to make effective contact with the attendees. Look at places other than your offices where you can hold the event and do it properly, and
- you can hold the session at a time and place that enough of your clients or targets can come – consider holding events near where your clients are rather than in your offices.

Get feedback forms filled in whenever possible and use them as a way of learning how to improve your events.

Attending events

Many of the issues are the same for events you attend:

- you need to have a genuine reason for doing so – you are interested in the topic, or have clients or targets that are interested in it.
- other people you are interested in are also interested. There are many ways of finding out information that are faster than attending events. If you do decide to go, make sure you arrive early enough to talk to the people who are your guests as well as the other people who attend. See if you can get there early enough to see the name tags and work out who will be attending.
- you have time. You will need enough time to look up information on the topic and time to spend talking with guests before and after the event. Obviously, you will need to be able to live with your phone off for more than five minutes, and
- be observant – see who is there, what level of people, what types of organisations. Notice what makes a good event and what makes a poor event, and make sure you use this information when you hold events yourself.

KNOW WHAT YOU NEED TO KNOW

About the process

- What's the background, why has this proposal come about (are there service issues associated with the incumbent/previous provider)?
- Who are the decision makers? (What are their respective roles, their individual agendas?)
- Who are the current providers?
- Which other firms have been invited to tender?
- What are the key selection criteria and which items will be given greatest importance?
- Will there be an opportunity to present to the client?
- What are the expectations in terms of the proposal document (style, level of detail, length)?
- What, in their opinion, will set us apart in our submission?
- What are the critical points that we would do well to cover thoroughly in the tender?
- Are there any other buying criteria that have not been outlined in the tender specification?

About the organisation

- What do they see as the principal three or four issues affecting their business and/or industry sector over the next 18 months to two years?
- What are the organisation's main strategic business priorities going forward?
- How would you describe the organisation's culture?
- Who are their major competitors?

About the team

- What are they looking for in a principal and team?
- Is the mix of experience and levels of staff appropriate to the work?
- How can we specifically and directly add value to their business?
- If we are appointed, how frequently would they wish to have contact/meet with the service team members, including formal service reviews?
- What is their preferred method of communication (meetings, conference calls, emails ,etc)?
- Is there a role for other practice groups – that is, a cross-sell opportunity?
- What KPIs would they see as being meaningful?

About the fees

- What fees are they paying now? (Some of this may be in their Annual Report, if they have one).
- What is their general expectation on fees?
- Can we explore various pricing approaches (fixed fees, success fees)?

WHAT TO DO NOW

- [ ] Review and improve your:
  - engagement and standard letters
  - invoices
  - publications
  - advertising
  - websites
  - technical papers/research
  - proposals
  - events

9 Business Development

Now you know what you want to promote and your target markets, make sure you use the resources of your staff and clients to grow your business.

WE HAVE already looked at some reasons and ways to identify, assess and rank your existing client base – both in terms of identifying your target markets and to maximise the value of your existing client relationships. Once you have these lists, you can also use them to assess the relative potential of your clients:

- which clients could you do more work for? Think about what is limiting that potential. Often it is as simple as asking the right questions and making sure clients know you have capacity and skills to do the work required.
- which clients have the ability to refer you work within their business group?
- which clients have the ability to refer you to other clients? This will be driven not just by their trust in you (see below) but also in their understanding of what services you offer.

Make sure all clients know everything you do

We often think of capability statements – in fact all marketing collateral – as material for new or potential clients. The truth is, if your business is driven by referral, then the best use of your marketing material is with existing clients.

Develop 'farming skills', for example checklists and client scripts that will help you discuss ways of maximising your potential with existing clients. List your major services and then match these against your clients. This helps you to know what services to talk about to which clients. If you cannot see what other services you can offer your clients, get someone else to look at your list for you.

Ask clients to be referrers – they are often the best judge of what you are good at, in which case you can use them to give you testimonials for proposals as well.

Client referrals

Client referrals are driven by two major factors: value and trust.

First, clients need to receive value from the work that you do for them and understand and be able to articulate what that value is. In order for this to happen, it is important that you discuss this with them so you *both* understand where you add value.

With trust, a client needs not just to think that you have done good work for her, but that she can trust you to deliver the same level of service to a colleague, so this enhances her reputation as well. In order for a client to stretch her own relationship by doing this, you need to gain that trust by being responsive and reliable. She needs to know that you can be relied on to do what you say you do.

A CAUTIONARY TALE

ONE firm could not work out why it was having trouble increasing the rate of referrals. They felt the general quality of their work was good and that clients were by and large happy with the work they did.

When we looked at their business development activities, it was clear they were spending a lot of time and effort courting new business through attending seminars, networking events, sponsorships, and so on. Like many other firms, they encouraged staff to record the amount of time they spend at these events. They even had a business development budget that each manager was expected to fulfil. At the same time, non-work or non-chargeable time spent with clients was treated as a write-off.

While mandating business development is a good idea, it focuses everyone's attention on the relatively difficult task of converting contacts into clients. What about growing work from existing clients? While everyone instinctively knew it was easier to get work from existing clients, in fact pressure on write-offs meant that this was discouraged. Essentially they were rewarding activities with strangers and discouraging spending time developing relationships with clients.

It is important to encourage and reward staff for the time they spend developing business with both potential *and* existing clients. The easiest way to do this is to allow new managers or associates to spend their time honing their talents on existing clients, then increase the time expected to be spent with potential clients. Establish a process where professionals meet on a regular basis to determine where their new work will come from. Some of this will be from existing clients, some from new clients.

Client referral will also be affected by:

- the level of involvement of the client in the service – the more involved they are, the more likely they are to refer, as the value of what you do for them is more obvious.
- the one-off or ongoing nature of the work – where your work is more one-off, the more dependent you will be on good levels of external (from non-clients) and internal (from staff) referrals. Here you will need to spend your time on business development with independent referrers as well as clients.

Get going

- analyse your client base
- establish the current level of client referral (how many clients come from other referrers, how many from tenders, how many from existing clients), and
- determine the extent to which you think it can be increased (for example, can you get to 80% referral?).

This can then form part of your marketing and business planning.

Once you have established which of your clients you most enjoyed working on and why, make sure they know you have enjoyed working with them and that you want to do more of it. At the very least it will make the client feel good and it may encourage them to give you more work! It will also encourage them to become ambassadors for your firm and to talk to their colleagues in other firms about you.

Business development from new clients

Once you have developed your target list you can then focus on identified industries and/or areas of business (associations, training, etc) of interest to you. Just as you have developed a marketing or business plan, so you can decide which of those targets you will be best to try to contact through networking. The main reason people are no good at networking is because they do not know what they want to achieve!

Develop a networking plan:

- What is the most successful way of getting new business (proposals, client referrals, etc)?
- Who do you want to meet (roles, industries, types of organisations)?
- · Where are they likely to be found (associations, business groups, locations)?
- What type of functions do these people hold (seminars, networking events, courses, etc)?
- What are they interested in (industry information, technical information, international contacts)?
- What work do you want to do for them when you have found them?

These do not need to be hard and fast rules, but as with speed dating, you need to know roughly what you are looking for so you will know when you have found it! Then you just need to practise talking about who you are and what you do and put yourself in the right places to meet them. Simple!

Networking tips

- identify people you know who are good at networking, look at what they do, ask how they do it.
- think about who you can give work to – you often need to give as a good way of receiving.
- distinguish yourself from others – have a way of describing what you do so you can be easily remembered.
- spend more time face-to-face with clients and each other in order to practise listening and talking about what you do.
- practise in-house first, then in a friendly group (university alumni, school reunions) before letting yourself loose on the real world.
- always carry business cards and a copy of your schedule.
- listen to what people say (do not just wait until they have finished talking so you can speak);
- don't just look interested, *be* interested.
- avoid standing with people you know all night at functions – make it a goal to meet new people, and
- keep track of what works and what does not – don't expect instant results. But also do not keep going to the same events if they are becoming a waste of time.

Staff referrals

Given that staff are every professional firm's greatest expense and investment, it is always surprising when you see how few referrals come from staff. There are a number of reasons for this, but the most common is that the partners (regardless of what they say) are unwilling, unable or afraid to let their staff get involved. This is a mistake:

Principals should always take someone with them to see the client. This not only means that there are two sets of eyes and ears at every meeting, but also that staff will begin to gain business development skills through observation. They will start to understand the types of people and organisations that make good clients, so they can identify them for themselves.

- a firm entirely dependent on the business development work of partners will always have difficulty managing its growth – when partners are busy then business development slows down and vice versa. Spreading the load makes good sense, and
- staff like to feel involved. It makes them feel more connected to the organisation. In this way, staff referrals can also form part of your staff retention program.

Business development is an essential part of any professional's skills. Training can give you the basics and some good hints, but is no match for in-the-field experience.

Encouraging your staff to refer work to you is a great way to give them some practical experience at a time when it is not as critical to their career as it will be later on. So how to get started?

Make sure staff know the type of clients you want

Sensible, but not that common! If you find it difficult to pull your head out of your work long enough to see where to go next, then imagine how hard it is for your staff. Make sure your staff know what type of clients you like, what type are the most profitable and what type of client or work you want more of.

Involve staff in meetings where you discuss your business development targets. Challenge and invite them to make suggestions.

Make sure staff know about the whole firm

One of the major barriers to business development is staff not knowing about the parts of the business they are not involved in. Make familiarisation with other sections of the firm part of your firm's induction, work patterns and/or training, so everyone in the organisation can describe not just what they do but what the whole firm does.

Most firms include cross-divisional training in their induction but it is important that all staff are given the chance to work and socialise together throughout their time with the firm at every level, so they know who to refer work to if ever the opportunity arises.

Practise talking about the practice

Even when everyone knows about the whole firm, you still need practice. Make sure you have a standard description of the firm that everyone can find and use, often called the 'elevator pitch' or the BBQ blurb. No one needs to memorise it or be able to recite it off by heart, but everyone needs to practise describing the firm when asked.

Everyone in the firm from the receptionist to the managing partner needs to be able to describe the firm and what you do.

Make sure all staff feel involved in the process

One of the greatest challenges facing firms is what happens when the second generation of staff starts to hit director or associate level.

The original principals that start a firm usually have the drive and the business development skills necessary to bring in business without thinking about it. The second generation consists, by definition, of employees, many of whom have had business brought to them by the principals. As they head toward the top, it seems all of a sudden they have to develop business development skills from scratch.

If this sounds familiar, it is – it happens in each 'generation' of the firm. In the second generation/cohort there will usually be a greater mix of business development and technical skills than in the first generation of principals. It is important then to get this group involved in the business development process as soon as possible.

Support staff (sometimes called non-professional staff, much to our chagrin) should also be encouraged to understand and be involved. They are often better at networking than the professional staff and, importantly, move in different and often wider circles.

Implement a staff referral program

At their most basic, staff referral programs reward staff for identifying people or organisations that become clients of the firm. Payments vary from one-off finders' fees to percentages of fees billed to the client. Regardless of how generous the staff referral program is, most firms find they cost very little. The reason for this is not the amount of money paid but the way that it is paid or administered.

Staff need to be encouraged to think of the firm intelligently and as early as possible. While it is sensible to stop paying incentives once business development is expected to be part of a person's everyday job, you can never start too early by encouraging and rewarding effort as well as outcomes. Encourage staff to always be on the lookout for potential clients. If they are unsure how to do it, make sure they feel comfortable enough to discuss the potential with someone.

It is important that *all* such ideas are treated seriously, regardless of how likely or unlikely it is that a suggestion will produce results. If all business development activity was only allowed or rewarded when successful, then no-one would ever have a go.

If a staff member has thought hard enough about the firm to identify a target, then all support should be provided to help them bring that client to fruition. If the client or the work is not appropriate, then they need to be helped to understand that, so they make a better selection the next time. Consider non-cash rewards for suggestions and ideas to show they are appreciated. Staff should also be encouraged to forge their own networks and develop relationships with their peers that will lead to referrals.

WHAT TO DO NOW

- [ ] Assess client referrals.
- [ ] Make sure clients know everything you do.
- [ ] Develop as much work with existing clients as possible.
- [ ] Develop a networking plan.
- [ ] Implement a staff referral program.

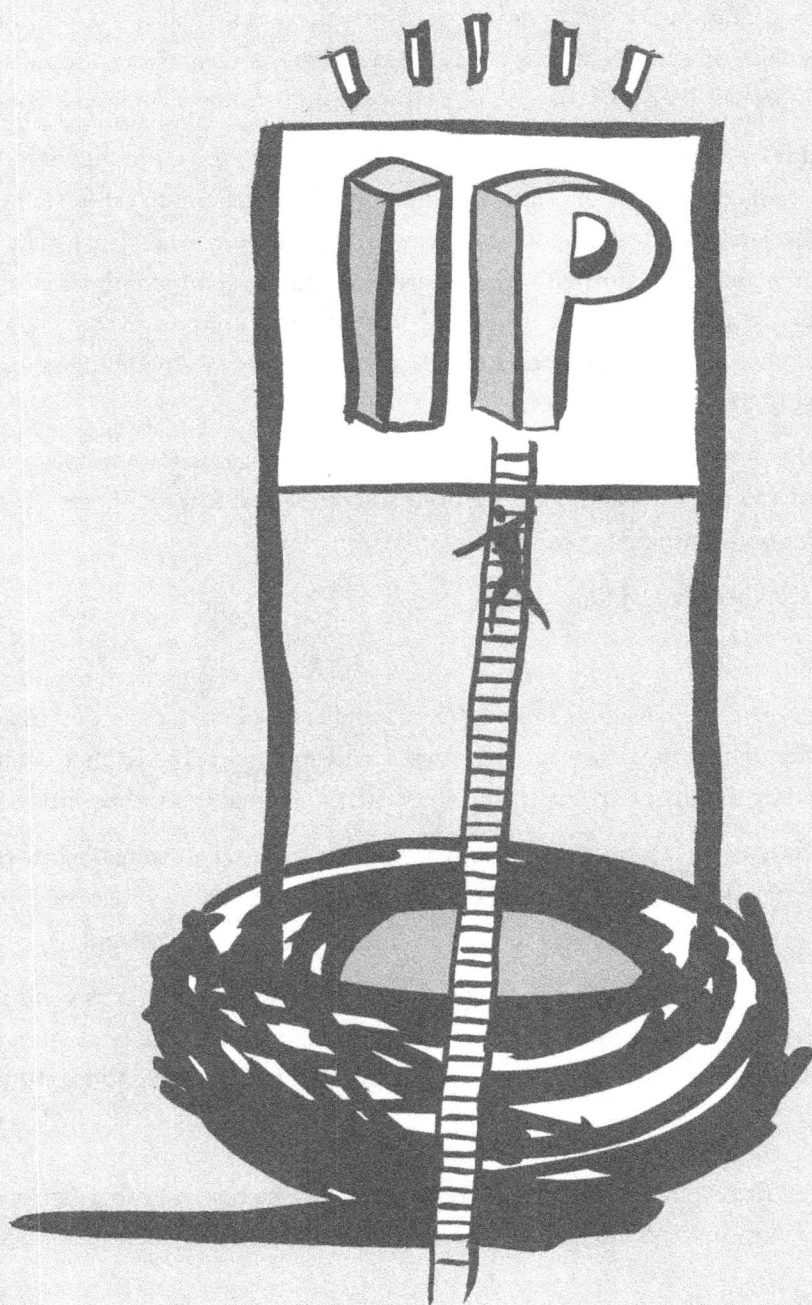

The value of your business may be between your ears, but you need to take a structured approach to protecting it, using it and maximising its worth.

T HE WHOLE concept of intellectual property (IP) and 'knowledge management' and all the other buzz words associated with these ideas send many professionals into a tailspin. Even in the largest firms there is a great deal of eyebrow raising and rolling of eyes about this issue. The principle is really quite simple – if you are in professional services, you charge people by the hour for applying what you know.

The real value of your business, then, is between your ears. Unfortunately, that is not a very safe place to store valuable information – it is difficult to replicate and sort and cannot be safely used when you are not physically present! Many of us like to think this is unchangeable – it reinforces our importance and the semi-magical way in which we are able to arrive at a solution. So if you like being indispensable, never going on holidays and being constantly at the beck and call of clients, read no further. For the rest of us, however, there are some options.

This is the point at which the words 'knowledge management', 'intranet', 'intellectual property' and even 'white paper' are used and strike fear into the heart of every good administration-loathing professional.

Take a deep breath and follow me.

Protect your assets

Recent court cases have highlighted the importance to architecture, design and IT companies of making sure that staff understand and agree that IP they create while they are employed by the firm remains the property of the firm and not their individual property.

While abuse of this process is rare, it is important that when valuable information is communicated to clients that both clients and staff understand that the information was created and is delivered by the firm and not the individuals involved.

Look at all the work you do for clients that you charge fees for. This work is one of your major assets and needs to be both protected and exploited. Get legal opinion if necessary to make sure your material is all properly attributed to the firm and can be protected.

Update

Most legal firms have well-established precedents systems and other firms could do well to learn from their example. The key thing is to make sure that all major opinions, plans, processes and methodologies are stored somewhere safe and secure but accessible by those who will need them. This is the key to efficiency and effectiveness. Well-catalogued and stored, this information can:

- save rework
- maximise the value of work done
- improve response times, and
- develop real technical depth.

One of the most common comments made by clients is that they see real value in learning from their professional advisers' other experiences. We all know this instinctively and will pepper our conversations about clients with similar situations or other solutions from other clients. The key, though, is to make this information more explicit so it can be used whenever you need to use it, rather than just when you remember it.

Make sure the information is saved in a way that it can be easily accessed. If you have an area of technical strength, make sure you keep the detail updated on a regular basis and that everyone who works in that area knows the practice is up-to-date. Set diary reminders to check on technical papers, standards, rulings, etc to make sure you stay at the top of your game.

In a single-office location this can be stored on the server or for multiple offices on an intranet. If you do not know how to develop multiple file names/indices for the one file then with the current cost of IT storage space it is probably cheaper to store multiple versions of the same file rather than try to develop a complicated referencing system.

Every time you or one of your colleagues learn something that is useful to a client, or even better learn something *from* a client, then it needs to be documented and stored. This is the first and most important step – you need to get yourself and your whole staff into the habit of writing things down and storing them somewhere accessible to someone else in the firm. Without an IT department or large administration team, you can do this yourself by having a process for naming, storing and retrieving it. Every time you finish a project, write down:

- what happened
- what went right
- what went wrong
- the value the client gained from the process, and
- what you would do differently next time.

This information needs to be stored by:

- client name
- industry
- type
- project type, and
- technical issue (if appropriate).

If the information you have just added to the system is important enough and/or affects a significant number of clients, then you need to tell everyone the information is there.

This might be an email or a list of new fields added each month. However you communicate it, it is not important that people know the detail of the file but that the file is there and exists, so they can find it when they need it. The important thing about this communication is that it needs to be fast and memorable (short emails, images, not long papers). Later on, this list of additions will form the basis of what needs to be included in technical training, and induction.

Make sure any new member joining the team gets to see and hear the whole history of the client and their relationship with your firm.

Maximise

Look at publishing this updated information both internally and externally and using it in communications with clients. Every time you spend a substantial amount of time on a matter, opinion or other piece of work, see what you can do to maximise the value of that investment. Who else in the firm should know about it, who else among your referrers or network would be interested, which of your clients and targets should be told? If it is of value to one client then much of the same information will be of use to someone else. You just need to make sure you get credit for it.

WHAT TO DO NOW
- [ ] Codify all regular processes.
- [ ] Store material somewhere secure.
- [ ] Make material accessible.
- [ ] Establish processes for adding and exploiting new learning.

11 Client Communication

Communication is a substantial part of your value to clients. Know what they want, when and how they want it — and don't raise expectations you can't meet.

ONE OF the first things we need to consider is what communication your clients want and how they want to receive it. Clients want to know what they are getting and given that the value they get from you is driven by the expectations you create, it is important you get this right. Clients want to be listened to and they value face-to-face and personal contact. They want communication during the project, not just at the beginning and the end of projects – simple, really!

In my experience, very few clients say they are being over-communicated with, so do not be afraid to start by asking them what they want. You can make this as formal or informal as you like, but you need to keep track of who wants what, when and how (Table 9). Do not assume you know all the stakeholders and what they think – they need to be treated as individuals. The important thing is to keep the information in a form easily accessible by everyone who comes into contact with the client.

For clients with multiple levels of contact, it is important to make sure that you have thought about each person at the client, what they are interested in and how they want to receive it. For privately owned businesses this may include family members not involved in the business on a day-to-day basis and for larger companies it may include investors. It may include other professional advisers. It is a good idea to establish a matrix (Table 9) of information about the client so you can see who wants to receive what, when and how.

For some of you, especially smaller firms and sole practitioners, you may be able to keep this in your head. For larger firms, though, you will need to keep the information somewhere that enables everyone who has contact with the firm to see it and update it if necessary.

When?

Set a timetable for communications so you make sure they receive some communication from the firm during the year. This is particularly important for those clients where you have only limited contact during the year – for example on audits, litigation or other one-off projects. Think of other things that may be of use or interest to the client throughout the year. Are there technical or industry issues that may be of interest? Are there social events or general communications you can use to fill the gaps?

Busy = Disorganised

Everyone is busy, including the client, but in the end, not talking to the client makes life more difficult for them and more difficult for you. Plan client contact throughout the job to keep everyone up-to-date.

TABLE 9: CLIENT INFORMATION

	MD	CFO	Accountant	Lawyer
Technical	N	Y	Y	N
General	Y	Y	N	N
Tax	N	Y	Y	Y
Industry issues	Y	N	N	N
Email	Y	Y	Y	N
Hard copy	N	Y	Y	Y
Social	Y	Y	N	N
Football	Carlton	Collingwood	Bulldogs	Melbourne

Even though they are busy, clients love unscheduled contact – they like to hear from or see you when it is not something they have requested or scheduled. The key, though, is that this contact needs to be unscheduled for them, not for you! You will need to know, and schedule to fill, the gaps in communication with your clients. Principals have a tendency to avoid communicating with clients as they get busy. Common excuses (and responses) include those in Table 10, next page.

While client communication needs to be the principals' responsibility, sometimes reminders are the best way of making it happen. Consider nominating someone else within the team as responsible for communication, for example, a manager, associate, PA or staff member who will be less easily ignored than electronic reminders and diary entries! This person can remind everyone, but *doing it* is everyone's responsibility.

What to say?

This will depend on your knowledge of the client and their interests. If you do not know, then it is simple enough to ask.

Work debriefs

A good place to start is with the work you have just done for them. If you have just finished a project, ask your team:

- what was the outcome of the project?
- what did we learn from the project?
- is there anything we could/should do differently next time?
- what was the real value of the project to the client?
- have we communicated this value to the client?

TABLE 10: COMMON EXCUSES FOR NOT COMMUNICATING	
Excuse	Response
I am too busy	Everyone is busy. If you do not communicate when you are busy then your clients will be targeted by people less busy (or more organised).
If I talk to them they give us work and we are too busy	Work is what you are in business for. Getting new work from existing clients is cheaper and easier than getting work from new clients. If you cannot take on new work, hold a crisis meeting and sort it out.
I do not have anything to say	You are their professional adviser, think of all the things you would have liked to discuss but have never had the time. See 'What to say', below.
They are too busy	There is no need to over-communicate. Even if clients are too busy to spend time with you, they do like to be asked.

Establish a meeting to have a proper debrief with the client. Make sure that everyone at the client firm knows this is taking place, even if it does not involve them directly. Think about the likely gap between this project or work and the next one. Is there a reason for you to get together with them in the intervening period? Can you do/report/say something that would be of value to them?

Work planning

If you have missed the opportunity for a debrief after a project (and often we all have, and want to move on to the next project), then schedule a meeting to plan for the next piece of work, at which you can pass on the same type of input and have some constructive discussion about the project.

Pass on client learning

Look at all the communication you have undertaken in the past month. If you cannot remember, have a look at your invoices – they should tell you what you have been talking to clients about. Somewhere in that list will be something that is also of interest to the client you have not spoken to.

If you have just been involved in a property deal, for example, think of all of your clients who might also be interested in what you have learned from that experience. Consider whether you want this communication to be a formal seminar or piece of paper, or whether a more informal email or chat would better suit you and the client.

Real value-add

What are the really critical issues affecting your clients and their industry? If you have not already found out, then this is the time to ask. There may be some industry or technical issues you need to keep on top of. Sources of useful information include:

- Google alerts
- industry magazines, websites or associations
- newsletters, and
- technical bulletins.

BEWARE THE EMAIL TRAP #3

WHAT to do with the information when you have it? We have all sent emails rather than ringing or meeting in person – it is faster, easier and requires no scheduling. But you only have to notice what you do with your own non-urgent emails to see what happens when you do this. If you are anything like me, you deal with the urgent ones and then save the others to review later, possibly even deleting them unread when things get really hectic.

Make sure email is not the only way you communicate important information to clients. Use email to confirm not inform.

Making client visits valuable

The important thing is to make sure client visits are valuable both for you and the client.

Have something to discuss: this is not the time to talk to them about technical issues – seminars or scheduled meetings at your office are better for that. The best subjects are those concerning their industry or type of business. You really only want a conversation starter.

Look, ask and listen: you can never know too much about a client's business. Make sure you make the most of every client visit. Ask for a tour of the operation if you have not had one already, and do the same for every new member who joins the team. Everyone loves to talk about their business and a tour is a great way to get them started.

> Never travel alone: visits to the client's office are a brilliant opportunity to introduce staff to the client and their operations. Even if your staff do not interact with the client on a regular basis, it will help them to get a deeper understanding of the client's business. Just as the more people you know at their business the better, so the more people the client knows at your end the better. Depth of client relationships is very dependent on numbers on each side of the relationship who know each other.

Meet and greet: meet their staff – not just the people you need to deal with on a regular basis but their operational staff. Develop a good relationship with the receptionist and all the personal assistants and administration staff. The more people you know in the business the better.

Unscheduled does not mean unplanned: in order for you to appear at the client on an unscheduled visit, you will need to plan your day to have some flexibility. You don't want to have to rush off, and you need to give the client enough notice that you are coming so their day is not interrupted. Unscheduled visits are driven by the desire to talk to the client, not necessarily by having something you need to do or discuss.

Think first: plan each visit to a client, discuss between you why you are going, what you want to achieve and importantly who is going to say and do what. Make sure you have a role for everyone who attends, even if it is noticing the environment and culture for later discussion. Confirm that the client is going to be there – you all need to look organised!

Managing internal communications

All too often the main problem in communicating with the client is communication within the firm. Even in small firms, it is not hard for everyone to be at cross-purposes over a client.

Background information

Make sure everyone who is working on a client knows as much about that client as possible. Who are they, what they do, how did they come to the firm, why do they stay? Are there issues in other countries or states we need to be aware of? What are the issues driving the client's business? Who owns the business, how is it structured or financed? Which other advisers is the client using, for what and why? If you do not know the answers to any of these questions, ask the client!

The bigger picture

It is very easy to focus on the work at hand, but we also need to think about the bigger picture and the way the client sees the work we do. What work do we do for the client, who does it and how is it delivered? There needs to be someone who takes overall responsibility for the client. For example, do we need to find another firm in the other jurisdictions in which they trade which can help them? Often, though, the help is closer at hand – has anyone else in our firm or network done similar work that would be of interest, or are there any other advisers or clients that we could introduce who would add value to the client?

Listen

It is also important to approach each project with a client as if they were a new client – do not take anything for granted. Look at what has changed since the last time we worked for the client, and listen to their expectations this time – are they different? Do not assume that every time we do work for a client it will be the same. Every time we need to confirm what they want, confirm what we are going to deliver and manage their team's expectations.

Passing on client learning

Sometimes we need to explicitly think about what it is that we can pass on to the client. If we did not have a chance to have a proper team debrief after the last job, then think before you start the next one – what did we learn from the last job, what went well, what could we have done better, what could they have done better?

One of the real reasons professionals can charge for their time is that they work with and learn from a number of clients. For clients to really appreciate and see the value in what we do, then we have to make this explicit. Is there anything we have done for another client that would help this client? Would they benefit from meeting with the other client?

Real value-add

- How can we really add value to the client?
- are there any issues we should raise that they would appreciate?
- are these issues worth sitting down and working through with them?
- are there team members who need to be brought up to speed? and
- how would we do that?

Client Communication Processes

The way in which clients are communicated with is driven by a number of issues, many of which are the ways in which we work with them.

One-off clients

- Think hard about longer-term resourcing to improve our chance of ongoing work with the client by maintaining the relationships
- meet face-to-face at the client's office to maximise the chances of developing a longer relationship
- confirm verbal discussion with engagement letters or contracts to make sure everyone understands what is expected and what will need to be delivered
- discuss a draft report before finalising the work with the client to confirm you have met expectations
- amend the draft report with client feedback to make the client see themselves as an essential part of the process
- include next steps in the report, where appropriate, to show you understand the broader context in which the work is delivered
- present it to all stakeholders, if possible, to maximise the effect
- communicate with the referral source about the project, to increase your chances of getting another one
- complete a project debrief with your team to identify what has been learnt, and
- file the debrief for future use (so you can find it!).

Project and intermittent clients

- Make sure you structure and maintain internal communications so you can pick up where you left off
- set up a three-year strategy and communication plan including a project-scope document, so you communicate even when there is no work on
- maintain contact between projects by running seminars and sending letters to clients on matters arising in other clients or in areas that might affect or interest them
- ensure information flows between all the divisions working on the client
- hold meetings on a regular basis to consider what else you could be doing for the client, and
- keep/file project notes up-to-date for other staff to see and use.

Ongoing clients

Oddly enough, it is often ongoing clients with whom communication is the worst. You take for granted that you will talk to them on a regular basis so you do not plan communications properly.

- Draft and revisit the engagement/retainer letter on a regular basis to make sure it spells out what you are doing
- make expectations and deliverables clear in the letter
- review whether you have the right team on an ongoing basis
- review with the team early on and on a regular basis
- document client progress to hand over to new team members
- call the client on a regular basis, if there is work or not
- maintain the relationship at all times
- schedule regular meetings and ensure you are meeting with the right people at the client
- follow up quickly on action items in writing after meeting with the client and the team
- arrange social functions with the client
- hold client team meetings on a regular basis
- ask the client for feedback on a regular basis, and
- be proactive.

All clients

- Develop a relationship map of who knows who
- document client history and progress to hand over to new team members
- make sure the client management system is up-to-date
- hold regular client meetings
- make sure letters are not the first time clients hear information or news
- practise effective listening with the client and team
- ask clients about their vision for the future
- look at future strategic issues, and
- treat old clients like new clients.

WHAT TO DO NOW

- ☐ Plan client communication.
- ☐ Plan what to say, to whom and when.
- ☐ Make every client visit valuable.
- ☐ Communicate appropriately with one-off, project and ongoing clients
- ☐ COMMUNICATE!

Work with Me

Hi, I am Vivienne Corcoran, the author of *Growing Your Professional Practice – The How-To Manual*. I specialise in helping professional practices of all kinds and sizes to grow and prosper.

I am available for:

- Strategy and growth consulting
- Professional development mentoring and coaching
- Business development training for marketing, business development and client facing staff
- Client engagement and service advice
- Marketing strategy, development and implementation
- Conference facilitation and speaking.

A selection of topics I have spoken on include:

- Starting your own business
- Building a career in professional services
- Building the practice you want
- Building effective teams
- Business development and client engagement
- Client service feedback – what do clients really want?
- Getting your practice known

- Identifying value in your practice
- Things women need to know to start their own businesses
- Communications in professional services
- Effective communications
- Finding your target market
- Marketing 101
- Presentation training and goal setting

Testimonials

'Vivienne's experience with professional firms meant she brought our leadership team together to agree on a Strategic Action Plan and has since developed and delivered focused training. The partnership group and the Firm are now very clear on what is needed for us to grow and thrive.' — David King, CEO, Robertson Hyetts Solicitors.

'Vivienne has been a major driver of our client service program. She has developed, gained support for and implemented client service initiatives across the firm. The client listening, feedback and service programs Vivienne developed are now an integral part of our business and a major driver of service improvement in our firm.' — Melanie Kent, National Marketing Director, Pitcher Partners.

'Vivienne has developed and delivered several training activities for our professional development programs. Each has been targeted, focused and engaging and the participant evaluations have been outstanding.' — Julie McCormack, Manager, Clinical Training Unit, Dental Health Services Victoria.

'Engaging, great interactive presentation.' 'Vivienne is a brilliant speaker, and clearly knows her skills and the market.' 'Very informative.' — Participant feedback from recent training sessions.

Contact me: vivienne@marketinglogic.com.au
www.marketinglogic.com.au
LinkedIn www.linkedin.com/in/viviennecorcoran
Twitter VivCor

marketing
Logic

NOTES

NOTES

NOTES